Presented By Commerce Enterprises INC
7950 NW 53rd Street
Suite 337
Miami, Florida 33166. United States.
+1 305 748-2021
sales@supreme-whip.com

Modernist Cooking Made Easy:
The Whipping Siphon

Create Unique Taste Sensations
By Combining Modernist Techniques
With This Versatile Tool

By Jason Logsdon

ISBN-13: 978-0-9910501-0-9 (Primolicious LLC)
ISBN-10: 099105010X

Other Books By Jason Logsdon

TABLE OF CONTENTS

FOREWORD: WHY THE WHIPPING SIPHON?

While I was working on my first book, *Modernist Cooking Made Easy: Getting Started*, I had the opportunity to play around a lot with a whipping siphon. I loved the different foams it could create and how easy it was to make flavored whipped creams. The more I looked into it, the more uses I found, including carbonating and infusing.

I was amazed at all the different ways a whipping siphon can be used to create unique taste sensations. From thick, rich foams to thin, flavorful froths and from fizzy grapes to highly-nuanced alcohol infusions, the whipping siphon can create food that plays with all of the senses. Plus, it was an awesome way to easily wow my family and friends!

However, while researching the whipping siphon I was struggling to find good, easy to follow information about how it works. There were numerous recipes but no explanation of how or why they worked. Once I finished with *Modernist Cooking Made Easy: Getting Started* I decided that my next book would be on the whipping siphon.

In this book, I've created the resource I wish I had last year when I was researching whipping siphons. It focuses on presenting the three main techniques the whipping siphon is used for: Foaming, Infusing, and Carbonating. It delivers the basic information you need to understand how the techniques work and provides you with numerous recipes to illustrate these techniques while allowing you to create dishes using them. Plus, these techniques can produce an amazing array of dishes that anyone can easily use to blow their diners away!

You can either go through this book from start to finish to gain a comprehensive mastery or you can use it as a handy reference and flip around to different chapters and techniques that currently interest you. I do recommend reading the Introduction to the Whipping Siphon section first since it will provide you with a foundation of knowledge required to understand the remainder of the chapters.

I have provided images of many of the dishes. For larger, full color images you can go to:

www.modernistcookingmadeeasy.com/whipping-siphon

To stay up to date with modernist cooking and what I am working on please:

Like my Facebook page at: www.facebook.com/ModernistCookingMadeEasy

Join my monthly newsletter at: http://eepurl.com/owpNb

Follow me on twitter at: @jasonlogsdon_sv

If you enjoy this book I'd love it if you took the time to leave a review on Amazon.com, the reviews always help other people decide if they want to purchase the book or not. Thanks!

Most importantly of all, remember to have fun!

SECTION ONE

INTRODUCTION TO THE WHIPPING SIPHON

Introduction to The Whipping Siphon

There is a lot to learn about using a whipping siphon. If you have any questions please ask them in the Modernist Cooking Forums on my website. Just post your questions and other cooks will weigh in with their answers.

You can find them on my website at:
www.modernistcookingmadeeasy.com/modernist-cooking-forums

The whipping siphon is a fun piece of equipment that adds many different textures to your cooking arsenal. At its most basic, a whipping siphon is a metal container used to pressurize liquids, typically with nitrous oxide (N_2O). This pressurization can be used for many different effects from foams and froths to carbonated foods and liquid infusions.

When a pressurized liquid is forced out the nozzle of the whipping siphon, the gas escapes from the liquid, aerating the liquid and turning it into a foam. The foam can range from a quickly dissolving froth to a heavy duty, dense foam through the addition of thickeners and stabilizers.

This same pressurization can also be used to infuse liquids with flavors or to marinate ingredients. Carbon dioxide (CO_2) can also be used in place of N_2O to carbonate liquids, sauces, or even fruits and vegetables.

How to Use a Whipping Siphon

It is surprisingly easy to use a whipping siphon. Place a liquid or fat into the whipping siphon. Seal the siphon by screwing the lid on, making sure all the pieces needed,

such as the gasket, are in place.

Charge the siphon by screwing in a gas cartridge or "charger". The charger holder can be left on or removed, whatever you prefer. Shake the siphon to help distribute the gas in the liquid.

The final step depends on the preparation you are making. For foams you turn the whipping siphon upside down, with the nozzle facing directly down, and pull the trigger to dispense the liquid through the nozzle for a foam or froth.

When making foams, some foam stabilizers will need to be heated or chilled before they are ready to be dispensed. This is covered in more detail in the Foaming Ingredients chapter.

For infusions and carbonation you vent the gas from the whipping siphon and strain the liquid remaining. To vent the whipping siphon, place the siphon upright, with the nozzle facing up, and place a towel over the top. Slowly pull the trigger and the gas should escape with a minimal amount of liquid.

Once you are finished with the whipping siphon make sure to clean it thoroughly. Most siphons come with good directions for how they should be cleaned. In general, take the siphon apart, wash the siphon and its parts in warm, soapy water, and use the scrubbing brush on the nozzle. Once the parts are clean, dry them well.

Nitrous Oxide vs Carbon Dioxide

The two main types of gas used with a whipping siphon are nitrous oxide (N2O) and carbon dioxide (CO2). Nitrous oxide is typically used to create foams and infuse foods while carbon dioxide is always used for carbonating.

N2O is more readily absorbed by fats and liquids. It also escapes from the liquid much faster and doesn't leave any trace that it was there. Conversely, CO2 becomes trapped in the liquid and escapes slowly, resulting in carbonation that adds a slightly sour or bitter flavor and a fizzy texture. Sometimes these effects are wanted and other times they are not.

While most CO2 and N2O is the same, some people have reported an off-taste in some gas chargers purchased through China. I always purchase my chargers through US or European companies where the restrictions are slightly higher.

Main Uses for a Siphon

There are three main uses for a whipping siphon that I cover. Each use has an entire section devoted to it later in the book.

Foaming

The most popular use for whipping siphons is to turn liquids into foams. These foams can range from light froths to heavy, creamy foams. This is almost always done with N2O unless you are making a sweet dessert foam and desire the fizzy texture from CO2.

Infusing

The whipping siphon is also great at infusing flavors into liquids. This can be used to infuse oil with herbs and spices, infuse fruits and vegetables with other flavors, and even to marinate meats. N2O is typically used for infusions.

Carbonating

Using CO_2 in the whipping siphon causes any liquid inside to become carbonated. This can be used to create sparkling drinks or even to carbonate the liquid in fruits and vegetables.

WHIPPING SIPHON TIPS AND TRICKS

Here are some of my tips and tricks for having a successful experience with your whipping siphon.

Don't Overfill

Make sure not to overfill the siphon. Most siphons have a fill-line on them that shows the maximum amount of liquid. If the siphon has too much liquid the foam won't have any room to expand and the gas will have trouble being absorbed.

Most siphons are named for the amount of liquid they are designed to work with. For example, a 1-pint whipping siphon is made to hold about 1 pint of liquid, even though the siphon itself is larger.

All the recipes in this book are written for a 1-pint whipping siphon. This size of siphon does best with 200 to 400 grams of liquid. If you have a larger or smaller siphon feel free to scale any of the recipes.

Always Vent Before Opening

Make sure you always vent your whipping siphon before you open it. Place the siphon upright, with the nozzle facing up, and place a towel over it. Slowly pull the trigger and the gas should escape with a minimal amount of liquid.

When in Doubt, Strain

When the foam is ejected from the whipping siphon it travels through a small nozzle. If there are particles in the liquid such as pieces of food, spices, or other non-liquid bits they can jam the nozzle and prevent the foam from coming out. The finer the strainer you use on the liquid the higher the probability that the foam will come out properly. I typically use cheese cloth, a chinois, or a fine strainer before foaming liquids with particles in them.

Double Check the Parts

Many siphons have several components that work together to make the seal. My iSi Whipping Siphon has a rubber gasket on the inside of the lid and the nozzle attachment holds the valve closed on the outside. Without both of these in place the gas quickly escapes the siphon. For example, sometimes after cleaning the siphon I forget to put the gasket back on the siphon and the gas leaks out when I try to charge it.

Use the Right Amount of Gas

Different size whipping siphons require different amounts of gas cartridges. Be sure to read your instruction manual to see what your siphon needs. While not typically dangerous, too much or too little gas will result in poor foaming and too much gas can freeze up the whipping

siphon, making it unusable. Typically a pint siphon uses one charger, a quart uses two, and a liter uses three chargers.

Check Your Heat Resistance

Some whipping siphons are designed to be heated. Make sure your siphon can be heated before following any recipes that call for heating or the addition of hot liquids.

Most of the recipes asking for a heat resistant whipping siphon can still be followed if you first cool the liquid or serve the foam cool instead of hot.

Always Clean Thoroughly

Thoroughly cleaning the whipping siphon is very important. Leftover foods and liquids in the siphon or nozzle can cause leaks that prevent the siphon from charging or foaming properly. For proper cleaning, see the manual that came with your siphon or the description under the How To Use title above.

Great for Storage

The lack of exposure to the environment makes whipping siphons great places to store the liquids you are foaming. Most liquids will last for a week or more inside the refrigerator in the siphon. In general, if you would feel fine storing the liquid in a container in the refrigerator, then it should be fine in the siphon in the refrigerator as well. The lack of air in the whipping siphon also slows browning of apples, avocado, and other items that can suffer from oxidation.

Use Finer Sugars

Often times you will want to sweeten a foam. Normal sugar works ok but superfine sugar or powdered sugar dissolve much more easily, especially when making whipped creams or using cold liquids. You can also use liquid sweeteners like agave nectar or simple syrups.

WHIPPING SIPHON TROUBLESHOOTING

Here are some common problems with whipping siphons and how to correct them.

The Foam Comes Out Watery

If your foam is coming out watery there are a few potential causes.

No Stabilizers

If the foam seems to come out ok but turns watery right away, make sure you have a stabilizer in it. Either some type of fat, or one of the ingredients discussed in the Foaming Ingredients chapter.

Leaking Gas

The gas might not be staying in your whipping siphon. Listen closely when you charge the siphon. After the initial rush of gas there should be no more noise. If you hear a hissing sound then you most likely have a leak. Vent your siphon and clean the parts. Double check that all the parts are there, especially the nozzle tip and the gasket. Then reassemble the siphon and try again.

To help find the leak you can try to submerge the whipping siphon in a tub of water and a stream of bubbles should quickly locate the area where the leak is occurring.

Improper Shaking

Make sure you are shaking the siphon before using it. This ensures that the N2O will be absorbed properly into the liquid. You typically want to shake hard three to five times. However, it is possible to over-shake liquids as well, though this results in a denser foam than desired.

Incorrect Gas Usage

Make sure you are using the correct amount of gas for your siphon size. Typically a pint siphon uses one charger, a quart uses two, and a liter uses three chargers.

Also double check that you are using N2O and not CO2, the chargers often look similar and can be confused with each other. N2O can also go bad, though this takes many years.

The Foam is Not Coming Out

There are a few things that can cause the foam to not come out of the whipping siphon.

Lack of Pressurization

A common reason foam doesn't come out is due to a lack of pressurization. First, ensure that there is still gas in the whipping siphon. Hold the siphon upright and place a towel over the nozzle. Depress the handle slightly until you hear a faint hiss of gas coming out.

If you hear the hiss, you may not have enough pressure. Make sure you are using the correct amount of gas for your siphon size. Typically a pint siphon uses one charger, a quart uses two, and a liter uses three chargers.

If the hiss of gas never comes, then either the siphon is not charged or it is clogged. If you are not sure if you charged it, try to add a new charge to it. If the gas still doesn't come out when checking, then the siphon is probably clogged. There a few causes of clogged siphons.

Too Thick of Liquid

If you have the correct pressure in your siphon then the liquid might be too thick. One cause can be over-shaking, you typically want to shake hard three to five times. If you let the liquid rest it can eventually loosen up.

This can also be caused by a stabilizer that thickened the liquid too much. To fix this you will need to vent the siphon, open it, and then thin the liquid inside using a less stabilized liquid or by blending it. Depending on the liquid, you can sometimes loosen it up by holding the siphon under warm water for several minutes.

Particles in the Liquid

If you have pressure and the liquid isn't too thick then a potential issue could be particles in the liquid are clogging the nozzle. These can be anything like bits of food, spices, or clumps of powders. You can try shaking the siphon to dislocate any particles. If this doesn't work then vent the siphon, strain the liquid through a fine sieve or cheesecloth, clear out the nozzle, and try to foam it again.

The Siphon Will Not Open

Make sure the whipping siphon has been properly vented or the pressure of the gas can make the whipping siphon very hard to open.

Sometimes the threads on the top of the whipping siphon will seize up, especially when it is cold. You can run it under warm water to try and loosen it up.

You Can't Vent the Siphon

Sometimes the siphon can get clogged, either from over charging it or through particles in the liquid clogging it. If it is due to particles you can try shaking the whipping siphon in different positions to clean up the nozzle.

If that doesn't work you can remove the nozzle attachment, place a towel over the siphon, and try to manually depress the nozzle. This can cause the siphon to dispense the gas, and probably a lot of liquid.

If the siphon is still stuck at this point I highly recommend contacting the customer service department for your whipping siphon.

The Siphon is Over Charged and Stuck

If you overcharge the siphon, the pressure inside can become too great. This pressure makes it impossible for the handle to move the nozzle enough to release it. There are some other ways to try to release the pressure. Read through the "You Can't Vent the Siphon" troubleshooter and see if any of those help.

The Siphon is Leaking

Sometimes there is hissing noise after the initial rush of gas when you charge your whipping siphon.

To try and fix this, first vent your siphon, then take it apart and clean it. Make sure all the parts are there including the gasket and the nozzle attachment. If this doesn't work then you likely have a defective gasket or nozzle head. The manufacturer of the siphon should have replacement parts for purchase.

The Foams Have an Off Taste

This is typically due to one of two issues. First, make sure you are using the correct type of gas, N_2O is usually flavorless while CO_2 can leave a bitter aftertaste. The cartridges can look the same and they are easy to confuse. If your foam has a bubbly, carbonated texture to it then it was foamed with CO2.

The second issue could be the type of N2O used. Some people have complained about some gas chargers produced in China that leave a bad aftertaste. Many people recommend only using chargers made in America or Europe. You may also be able to solve this by purchasing a filtering kit such as the NitroKit from Creamright.com.

The Gas Stays in the Charger

Sometimes when you try to charge your whipping siphon the gas will stay in the charger. This is usually due to an issue with the pin that pierces the canister. Replacement pins can usually be purchased from the manufacturer.

ABOUT THE RECIPES

Due to the wide range of whipping siphons available I've made a few assumptions in the recipes. Here they are so you can adjust the recipes as needed to work with your siphon.

Hot Liquids

Many recipes call for pouring a hot liquid into your whipping siphon or heating the whipping siphon in a water bath. Only do this if you have a whipping siphon that is able to withstand heat. Non-heat resistant whipping siphons can be damaged by excessive heat. Many of the recipes in this book that use a heat resistant whipping siphon will work fine if you let the liquid cool first and serve the foam cool.

Siphon Size

All recipes in this book are for a 1-pint whipping siphon. They should also work fine in larger siphons but must be reduced for smaller siphons. All recipes are given in grams and can be easily scaled up or down as needed.

Charge Amount

All recipes have you "charge" the whipping siphon. Unless otherwise noted, this refers to a standard charge of nitrous oxide for your brand and size of whipping siphon. You should be able to find what a standard charge is in the instruction manual that came with your siphon. Typically a pint siphon uses one charger, a quart uses two, and a liter uses three chargers.

Variations

All of these recipes are suggestions for the foaming ingredients to use and most are interchangeable. For example, the Jamaican Jerk Foam creates a thick, dense foam. But if you wanted a froth you could omit the agar and just use xanthan gum, keeping the rest of the recipe the same.

Making Gels

Many of the recipes, especially using agar or carrageenan, say "pour into a container and let set". I often get asked what type of container to use. Since after it sets you will be blending the gel, the type of container doesn't matter too much. I tend to use a tall, cylindrical container so I can use my immersion blender directly in it but you can always transfer the gel to a new container, or a standing blender, before blending.

Straining Liquids

Many recipes call to strain the liquid before putting it into the whipping siphon. As mentioned in the Tips and Tricks, this is due to particles in the liquid clogging the whipping siphon. You can use a chinois, cheesecloth, or other strainer to accomplish this. The finer the strainer used, the finer the foam will be.

SECTION TWO

FOAMING

FOAMING PRIMER

I am constantly adding recipes to my website as I continue to experiment with modernist cooking.
Maybe something there will inspire you.

You can find them at:
www.modernistcookingmadeeasy.com/info/modernist-recipes

Probably the most popular application for a whipping siphon is making foams. There are several types of foams you can make that range from wet and light, like froths, up to dense foams like traditional whipped cream. Because foams are such a large part of using a whipping siphon I wanted to include a primer on what foams are and how they are made.

WHAT ARE FOAMS?

Foams are one of the techniques most associated with modernist cooking. They are easy to make, very versatile, and fun to use and eat. Foams have been around traditional cooking for a very long time and include whipped cream, head on beers, and even bread dough.

At the most basic level, foams are structures that trap air in bubbles or pockets. Foams are similar in this way to emulsions, which occur when liquid traps fat in a structure, or fat traps liquid in a structure.

The structure can be made from a variety of things such as proteins, water, or fat. The texture of the foam is determined by the size of the bubbles, how much liquid is in the foam, and what the structure is made from.

Most foams eventually collapse when all the air escapes or the structure breaks down. However, some foams are considered "set" foams, which means the structure has been solidified, such as when baking bread dough or dehydrating a meringue.

HISTORY OF FOAMS

The first common use of culinary foams dates back to the 1700's when both sweet and savory soufflés were created. The name soufflé literally translates to "puffed up", which is a description of the dish and the soft matter which is neither flowing nor completely solid. The use of foams evolved to meringues and eventually the cream that is put in many gourmet beverages today.

In the world of molecular gastronomy, foams have evolved into a completely new cooking technique as well. Much of the change in how foams are used and prepared can be credited to Spanish chef Ferran Adría. In his efforts to enhance the flavor of food, Adría eliminated the use of cream and eggs in his foams, opting for other, milder stabilizers that would let the base flavor of the liquid come through more strongly.

Culinary foams are often created with familiar flavors taken from stock, fruit juices, vegetable purees and even soups. These are combined with stabilizing agents to prevent breakdown of the foams later on. Stabilizers are usually from natural plant and animal derivatives. Examples of commonly used stabilizers are agar, xanthan gum, carrageenan, and soy lecithin. Depending on what is being made, fats and egg whites may also be used.

Air is then introduced into these through a mechanical force in the form of whipping. Foams made with the use of a hand held immersion blender results in a delicate froth similar to that found in cappuccino. On the other hand, those made with a whipping siphon result in a range of foams from froths to dense foams comparable to mousse.

In the same way that traditional foams can be made either sweet or savory, so can modern cuisine foams. They can also be served in a range of temperatures from cold to hot.

USES OF FOAMS IN CUISINE

Adding Taste with Foams

Like many other molecular gastronomy techniques, foam serves a number of purposes that all point to giving its audience a better dining experience. Flavor is one of the most important functions that foam carries in the kitchen. It allows cooks to incorporate various tastes into dishes being cooked without changing physical makeup. Foam can simply be added on top of a completed dish and it will deliver the desired flavor.

Presentation with Foams

Without any doubt, culinary foams also play a large role in the way a dish looks when it is served. Long before the advent of modern cooking, foams had already served to make dishes look much more appetizing. With the use of new approaches and equipment in creating these airy substances, the options for creating enticing dishes are widened.

Creativity with Foams

One of the things that can make dining more enjoyable is the experience of new things. Foams make it possible for diners to feel different textures in their mouth. This is especially true when it is combined with other foods that offer contrasting textures. It also allows for the use of unorthodox cooking methods such as the formation of sauces and even warm foams.

Preservation with Foams

On a more industrial level, the production of foams with the use of a siphon makes it possible to store these substances longer. Modern cuisine foams have an extended shelf life and are not susceptible to absorbing smell and taste from other foods due to storage options. This means better tasting and fresher dishes will be served to diners.

SPECTRUM OF FOAMS

Whether they are called bubbles, airs, meringues, espumas, puffs, or froths, all foams share certain characteristics. These characteristics aren't absolutes but lie on a spectrum.

Fine vs Coarse Foams

The texture of a foam ranges from fine to coarse and refers to the size and uniformness of the bubbles.

A foam with smaller, very uniform bubbles is considered fine. Whipped cream is an example of a fine foam. A foam with larger and less uniform bubbles is considered coarse. Some examples of coarse foams are latte froth, airs, and the head on light beer.

Dry vs Wet Foams

The wetness of a foam refers to the amount of liquid that is in the structure of the bubbles. Usually, the coarser a foam the dryer it is.

Dry foams are mainly air and can be very light. The bubbles are typically larger and their flavor is diluted due to the lack of liquid. Most very dry foams are referred to as "airs".

Wet foams have much more liquid in their structure. They can range from light to dense foams. They are usually fine foams, rather than coarse foams. Most commonly known foams are wet foams such as whipped cream and milkshake froth.

Airy vs Dense Foams

Foams can range from very light, such as airs, to very dense, mousse-like foams similar to whipped cream. The density depends on the texture and wetness of a foam. The finer the bubbles are and the wetter the foam is, the denser it becomes.

TYPES OF FOAMS

There are different names for types of foams. Some of these are interchangeable and none of the definitions are set in stone. To understand what people are referring to when talking about foams, it's important that you learn the characteristics associated with the following names.

Airs

Typically a dry, coarse foam that is mainly made up of air. Strongly flavored liquids should be used in airs because they have such a small amount of liquid in the bubble structure.

Dense Foams

Dense foams refer to thicker, fine, wet foams. They usually have smaller bubbles. Whipped cream is a good example of a dense foam.

Light Foams

Light foams lie somewhere in between airs and dense foams. They are finer and wetter than airs but not as thick as dense foams.

Bubbles

Like airs, bubbles are coarse foams but they tend to have more liquid in them than airs do and are made up of larger bubbles. They usually resemble common bubbles like those created by soap or shampoo.

Froths

Froths are usually wet but coarse foams. They are named after the froth that is often on the top of a milkshake or latte.

Set Foams

Set foams have had their structure solidified, often through heating or dehydrating. A loaf of bread and a dehydrated merengue are examples.

Espumas

"Espuma" is the Spanish word for foam and they are usually dense foams. They are always created by a whipping siphon and usually served hot.

Meringues and Puffs

Meringues and puffs are lighter foams that are often baked or dehydrated to set their structure.

STABILIZING FOAMS

In order for a foam to last more than a few seconds it needs to be stabilized. There are many ways to stabilize a foam, often by thickening or gelling the liquid.

Thickened Liquid Foams

One of the simplest ways to create a foam is to combine a liquid with a thickening ingredient, such as xanthan gum. Then you introduce air into it, usually through whipping, blending, or using a whipping siphon. This typically results in a coarse, wet foam that is on the lighter side.

Xanthan gum is usually added in a 0.2% to 0.8% ratio, depending on the density of foam desired.

Stabilized Foams

Similar to thickened liquid foams, stabilized foams combine a stabilizer such as lecithin or Versawhip with the liquid. The resulting foam tends to be a little finer than thickened liquid foams. These can usually be made with most of the foaming equipment listed in this article.

Using traditional stabilizing agents like egg white, cream, and sugar are also effective. Many of the things in those ingredients that stabilize the foam have been isolated and are sold as separate ingredients, such as lecithin. These are also incorporated into other modernist ingredients such as Versawhip.

A ratio of 0.5% to 1.0% is commonly used for Versawhip. Lecithin is used at a 0.25% to 1.0% ratio. Xanthan gum can also be added to the above ingredients to thicken the foam at a ratio of 0.1% to 0.5%.

Gel and Fluid Gel Foams

An effective way to create thicker foams is by using gels and fluid gels. You first turn the liquid you want to foam into a gel. Agar agar, iota carrageenan, gelatin, or methylcellulose are often used to create the gel, or fluid gel. Depending on the ingredient, the gel can be whipped or put in a whipping siphon to create a foam. These foams have a range of textures and densities depending on the fluid gel used.

Agar fluid gels are usually made with a 0.25% to 1.0% ratio. Gelatin is used with a 0.4% to 1.7%. Xanthan gum can also be added to the above ingredients to thicken the foam, typically in a 0.1% to 0.4% ratio.

FOAMING EQUIPMENT

There are many tools you can use to create foams and each one results in a slightly different texture. The purpose of all the tools is to introduce air into the liquid you are foaming. For tools such as whisks and immersion blenders you want to make sure part of the tool is out of the liquid so it will carry air into the foam.

Whisks, Manual and Electric

Whisks are a great way to create dense foams as well as some lighter foams. Manual whisks can get the job done but using an electric whisk attachment greatly speeds up the process and tends to make finer foams. The whisk attachment can be on an immersion blender or a standing mixer.

Whipping Siphon

The whipping siphon is a great tool for making foams of all kinds. Whipping siphons are very effective at creating foams and also help in the storage of liquids you will be foaming over time.

Standing or Hand Held Mixer

Mixers without a whisk attachment can also be used. They can create lighter foams very efficiently.

Milk Frother

A milk frother is an inexpensive tool that is used to create foam for cappuccinos or lattes. When it used with modernist ingredients it can create similar foams from other liquids. Aerolatte brand frothers are usually under $20.

Immersion Blender

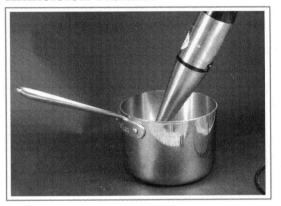

Immersion blenders are good at creating airs and other light foams. Ensuring part of the blade is out of the liquid is critical. A traditional standing blender will not work well for foaming because the blades are completely submerged.

Aquarium Bubbler

An aquarium pump or bubbler is one of the more unusual ways to create foams. It works well for creating large bubbles, similar to soap bubbles. Tetra Whisper brand pumps can typically be found for under $10.

OTHER USEFUL EQUIPMENT

Scales

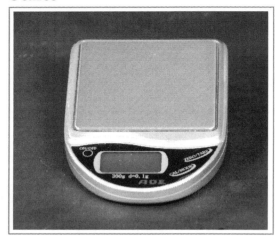

There are two types of scales needed for most modernist cooking. A gram scale, for weighing out small ingredients and a kilogram / pound scale, for measuring large amounts of an ingredient.

I recommend electronic versions of each scale, they tend to be much more accurate and allow you to easily tare (reset) the scale so ingredients can be added into the same bowl.

The kilogram / pound scales typically increase in increments of 1 gram which works well. A maximum weight of at least 2,250 grams / 5 pounds is ideal, and I prefer one with at least 10 pounds so I can easily weigh larger amounts of food.

For the gram scale, an increment of 0.1 grams is normally good enough. Some scales increase by 0.01 grams, which is just fine, but probably a bit of overkill for most applications. The max weight is less important on the gram scale since most are above 100 grams.

Weighing Dishes

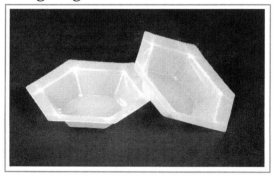

There are many types of dishes used in weighing, especially in weighing the small amounts of powder used in many modernist recipes. They typically are anti-static and the powders don't stick to them as much as some other containers. They come in a few sizes and I recommend getting a few of each size. They will make measuring a lot easier and they usually are less than a dollar apiece.

If you don't want to get the dishes it can be useful to measure the powders on a piece of paper since they won't stick to it as much.

Silicon Molds

Silicon molds are a great way to create unusual shapes with your frozen foams. They are inexpensive and come in a wide variety of shapes. I prefer them to the more rigid plastic molds because the frozen foams can be very delicate and the flexible silicon makes the unmolding easier.

Standing Blender

I love my immersion blender and use it with most preparations but sometimes I need the added power of a standing blender. It is much better at breaking down vegetables for purees and for crushing ice.

Strainer / Chinois

A chinois is a fine, metal strainer. It is great for removing pulp from purees and other liquids. You can use something like cheesecloth for many preparations but a chinois makes the process easier in many cases.

Isi also sells a combination sieve and funnel that works great as well.

Juicer

Juicers can be pretty expensive but if you regularly make foams they can greatly expand your options. Fruit and vegetable juices can be used with many modernist techniques to create gels, foams, and sauces. You can make juices with blenders and food processors but a juicer is more efficient and often easier to use.

FOAMING INGREDIENTS

Did You Know: I have a fan page on Facebook and a twitter account. You can follow me there for updated recipes, tips, and equipment reviews.

You can find them at:
www.facebook.com/ModernistCookingMadeEasy
and twitter.com/jasonlogsdon_sv

FOAMING RATIOS AT A GLANCE

Agar
Light Foam: 0.3%-1.0%
Dense Foam: 1.0%-2.0%

Gelatin
Sheet Gelatin (per 100 grams of liquid)
Light Foam: 0.2-0.55 sheets
Dense Foam: 0.55-0.9 sheets

Powdered Gelatin
Light Foam: 0.4%-1.0%
Dense Foam: 1.0%-1.7%+

Mono and Diglycerides
For oil and fats
Light Foam: 2.0%-5.0%
Dense Foam: 5.0%-10.0%

Iota Carrageenan
Light Foam: 0.2%-0.75%
Dense Foam: 0.75%-1.0%

Ultra-Sperse
Froth: 0.2%-3.0%
Light Foam: 3.0%-5.0%

Ultra-Tex
Froth: 1.0%-4.0%
Light Foam: 4.0%-8.0%

Versawhip
Often with 0.1%-0.2% xanthan gum added
Froth: 0.5%-1.0%
Light Foam: 1.0%-2.0%

Xanthan Gum
Froth: 0.2%-0.5%
Light Foam: 0.5%-0.8%

There are two main components to every foam. The flavoring ingredient and the foaming ingredient. The flavoring ingredient is what brings all the flavor to the foam while the foaming ingredient determines what type of foam you will create.

COMMON FLAVORING INGREDIENTS

Most foams start out as a flavored liquid that is turned into a foam. These liquid bases can be about any flavored liquid and they can be tailor-made to match the dish you want to serve them with. Part of the fun with modernist cooking is experimenting with different flavors and there are lots of ways to create these flavored liquids.

Citrus Juices
Most citrus juices work well as airs and light foams. You may want to

add some sugar or water to help balance out the flavors.

Pre-Made Sauces

Most pantries contain many pre-made, strong sauces that work great as foams. Soy sauce, mirin, or fish sauce components make great light foams on Asian-inspired dishes. Worcester sauce, steak sauce, and thin vinegar-based BBQ sauce based components add texture and flavor to steak, pork, and chicken. Heavier sauces like sweet BBQ sauce, hoisin sauces, or teriyaki sauce can easily be used as heavy foams.

Vinegars

Vinegar is often used in a dish or sauce to add brightness and acidity. You can take that same concept but use the vinegar to create a flavorful component to also add visual appeal to the dish. You may want to add some sugar or water to the vinegar to balance the flavor if it is too strong.

Vegetable and Fruit Juices

A favorite foaming ingredient of mine is vegetable or fruit juice. If you have a juicer or good blender, making your own juice is easy, otherwise many grocery stores sell a variety of natural juices. If there are lots of particles in the juice then be sure to strain it through a chinois or cheesecloth.

These foams can be added to traditional dishes for a dramatic flavor and visual effect. Some great pairings are apple cider on pork chops, carrot on peas and pancetta, or a cranberry on turkey.

Brewed Liquids

Coffees and teas open up a wide range of liquids and flavors you can use in your dishes. Brew the coffee or tea then turn it into a foam and add it to dishes. From the whimsical, like orange-peppermint air on cake, to the hearty, like french roast coffee foam on steak, you have many interesting options.

For another take on teas, you can create your own tea by steeping herbs, spices, and aromatics in hot water. I really enjoy thyme and rosemary air on pork, juniper and thyme foam on duck, or orange peel and fennel froth on salmon.

PICKING FOAMING INGREDIENTS

One of the most common questions I get asked is, "Which ingredient should I use to make a foam?" It's a really difficult question to answer because there are so many different variables that go into it. However, most of the differences between the foams produced by the ingredients are very subtle, which makes it easy to substitute one ingredient for another until you learn the specific differences.

I've found there are a few major considerations you need to take into account. Any ingredient that fulfills all of them should work well. As you become more experienced with making foams you will start to notice the smaller differences between ingredients and can adjust accordingly.

Hot vs Cold

One thing to determine is if the foam will be served on a hot dish or a cold one. The foams from several ingredients will break down at high temperatures. Some ingredients that work well with heat are agar, iota carrageenan, xanthan gum, mono and diglycerides, low-acyl gellan, and Ultra-Sperse.

Light vs Dense Foams

Most ingredients can successfully create light foams. However, for dense foams, some do a better job than others. Agar, iota carrageenan, mono and diglycerides, low-acyl gellan, and gelatin are all good ingredients to use for denser foams. For light foams you can use smaller amounts of those. Xanthan gum, Versawhip, soy lecithin, and Ultra-Sperse are also all good for creating light foams.

Liquid Being Foamed

Some liquids are best foamed with certain ingredients. To foam oil it is best to use mono and diglycerides. Liquids with fats in them can't be foamed with Versawhip. Liquids you do not want to heat shouldn't use agar, carrageenan, or gelatin because they have to be heated to be activated.

So when trying to determine an ingredient to use, just make sure it works in those categories and you really can't go wrong.

Below is an extended look at many of the foaming ingredients you can use. For a generalized and more detailed look please reference my comprehensive book *Modernist Cooking Made Easy: Getting Started*.

USING FOAMING INGREDIENTS

Before I jump into the foaming ingredients there are a few important concepts I want to review.

Modernist Terms

There are a few concepts used in modernist cooking, and actually in all cooking, that are critical to understanding how the recipes will work.

Dispersion

Dispersion refers to the process of evenly distributing one ingredient into another one. Proper dispersion is critical to ensure the ingredient affects all of the mixture it is going into instead of forming clumps.

Different ingredients are dispersed in different ways. For instance, sugar is easily dispersed in hot water while flour will form clumps. Most foaming ingredients are easily dispersed in a cold liquid with a standing or immersion blender. If there is a better way to disperse it I will describe it in the ingredient's section below.

Hydration

Many of the ingredients need to be hydrated before they will work. Hydration is simply the process of adding water to the ingredient. Often you also need to bring the liquid to a specific temperature to ensure the ingredient will hydrate properly. For instance, after you add flour to water to make a gravy you have to heat it up before the flour will thicken it.

This is also true of many baking preparations, such as letting popover dough sit for 30 minutes for the flour to fully hydrate.

For each ingredient below I describe the best way to hydrate the ingredient.

Proper Weighing

To someone not familiar with using a scale it can be a little intimidating until you use it once or twice. The main concept of using the scale is learning to "tare" or "zero" the scale. All digital scales will have a "tare" / "zero" button. What this does is reset the weight to zero.

This allows you to measure all the ingredients in the same bowl. You simply turn on the scale and place the bowl on it. Hit the tare button so it resets to zero. Add the next ingredient, then tare it to zero again. Repeat for all the ingredients.

You will most likely have to use a larger scale for the liquids or main ingredients and a smaller gram scale for the modernist ingredients.

Ingredient Ratios

Many of the ingredients will specify the ratio they should be used in. All the ratios refer to the weights of the ingredients. For example, an agar recipe might say to add 2% agar. The 2% means that the weight of the agar should be 2% of the weight of the liquid it is being added to. So if you had 300 grams of fruit juice you would add 6 grams of agar to it, or 300 x 0.02.

AGAR FOAMS

Agar foams are made from an agar fluid gel. They typically range from light, coarse foams to dense, fine foams. One big benefit of agar foams is that they can be used in hot or cold preparations so you will often see them on savory, hot dishes.

To make an agar foam, combine a liquid with agar using an immersion or standing blender, bring it to a boil for 3 to 5 minutes, then let it cool into a gel. Blending that gel turns it into a fluid gel. This fluid gel is added to the whipping siphon which is sealed and charged.

The more agar you use the denser the resulting foam will be. For light foams, a ratio of 0.3% to 1.0% works well. For denser foams 1.0% to 2.0% is recommended. You can also add gelatin, locust bean gum, or xanthan gum to change the density and coarseness of the foam.

Quick Recipe: Agar Mango Foam

Pour 400 grams of fresh mango juice into a pot and add 2.0 grams agar (0.5%) to it. Blend well with an immersion blender. Bring to a boil and let simmer for 3 to 5 minutes. Remove from the heat, pour into a container, and let cool.

Once cool, use a standing or immersion blender to blend the mango agar gel until smooth. Add to a whipping siphon, seal, and charge.

This foam can be used both on hot and cold dishes.

Dairy Foams

There are a wide range of dairy foams you can make. They are usually made with cream or a soft cheese, such as cream cheese or mascarpone.

Most cream foams are heavy, dense foams but they can also be used for lighter foams. The most commonly used cream-based foam is whipped cream.

At its most basic, whipped cream is simply heavy cream whipped until it stabilizes and forms peaks. The caseins and proteins in the cream act as foaming agents. Adding additional stabilizers, such as sugar or xanthan gum, to the cream can help in the foam creation.

Quick Recipe: Whipped Cream

Pour 225 grams (1 pint) whipping cream into a whipping siphon and add 16 grams powdered sugar. Seal the siphon and charge it. Shake hard three to five times and dispense the whipped cream.

For additional flavors you can add flavored extracts or juices to the siphon. The whipped cream in the

siphon can be refrigerated for several days.

Egg Foams

When eggs are cooked and blended they form a fluid gel. This fluid gel can thicken and stabilize foams.

The eggs are usually cooked for 35 minutes at 60°C / 140°F to 80°C / 176°F depending on the thickness of the fluid gel you want to create. The eggs can also be separated to control the amount of yolk and white used in a foam. Occasionally egg foams will not set properly when hot. In this case you can cool them in the refrigerator until they set and then re-heat them.

Both the yolk and white of eggs can be used to stabilize foams, though they behave and taste differently. When yolks are used the flavors are very pronounced, while whites fade more into the background. Here is an example of two very similar recipes that result in very different foams, one with egg whites and one with egg yolks.

Quick Recipe: Maple Egg Yolk Foam

Blend 200 grams of egg yolks, place in a sous vide bag and seal. Cook for

35 minutes in a 70°C / 158°F water bath. Remove from the bag and blend with 10 grams maple extract until smooth. Strain into a whipping siphon, seal, and charge. You can heat the sauce as long as you do not go above the initial cooking temperature and you have a heat resistant whipping siphon. Dispense to serve.

Quick Recipe: Maple Egg White Foam

Blend 200 grams of egg whites and 100 grams sugar then place in a sous vide bag and seal. Cook for 35 minutes in a 75°C / 167°F water bath. Remove from the bag and blend with 12 grams maple extract until smooth. Strain into a whipping siphon, seal, and charge. You can heat the sauce as long as you do not go above the initial cooking temperature and you have a heat resistant whipping siphon. Dispense to serve.

GELATIN FOAMS

Gelatin foams range from light and airy to heavy and dense. All gelatin foams have fine, evenly distributed bubbles. Gelatin foams must be served cold or they will break down and melt. The addition of agar can help strengthen gelatin foams.

For light foams, powdered gelatin in a 0.4% to 1.0% ratio work well. For denser foams, using powdered gelatin in a 1.0% to 1.7% ratio is typical. Sometimes you will see even higher ratios.

If you are using sheet gelatin you would normally use 0.2 to 0.55 sheets per 100 grams of liquid for light foams or 0.55 to 0.9 sheets per 100 grams of liquid for dense foams.

To make a gelatin foam, first hydrate the gelatin then disperse it into the liquid you want to foam. Pour the mixture into the whipping siphon and refrigerate it for several hours so the gelatin can set before dispensing it.

For additional information about hydrating, dispersing, and converting between types of gelatin please see "How to Use Gelatin" in the References section.

Quick Recipe: Gelatin Cider Foam

Place 400 grams of cider into a pot with 2 gelatin sheets or ½ packet of gelatin (0.9%). Let it bloom for 5 to 10 minutes then, while stirring, heat the pot over medium heat until the gelatin dissolves.

Pour the cider mixture into a whipping siphon, charge, and shake several times. Refrigerate for several hours, at least 2 to 3, until the gelatin sets. The foam will now be ready to dispense.

MONO AND DIGLYCERIDES FOAMS

Mono and diglycerides thicken and emulsify oils. This makes them very effective at creating oil foams.

They are high stability emulsifiers composed of monoglyceride and diglyceride taken from the fats of glycerin and fatty acids. Despite commonly being called "glycerin flakes", they do not actually contain any glycerin.

In order to disperse the mono and diglycerides you have to heat the oil above 60°C / 140°F, at which point they melt and can easily be stirred in. Once they have been dissolved, the oil can be added to a whipping siphon, sealed, charged, and dispensed. The foam thickens as the oil cools, so for thicker foams you can refrigerate them.

The more mono and diglycerides you use the thicker the resulting foam will be. Typically 2.0% to 10.0% is used for foams.

Quick Recipe: Sesame Oil Foam
Combine 215 grams of sesame oil with 16 grams of mono and diglycerides. Heat the oil until the mono and diglycerides melt. Remove from the heat and let cool to room temperature. Pour into a whipping siphon, seal, and charge. The foam is then ready to be dispensed.

IOTA CARRAGEENAN FOAMS

Iota carrageenan foams are made from fluid gels, similar to agar foams. They can be used in hot or cold preparations, though they are firmer when cold. Iota carrageenan works especially well with dairy based products.

To make an iota carrageenan foam, combine the iota carrageenan with the liquid you want to foam. Bring the mixture above 70°C / 158°F, or as high as a boil, then pour the liquid into a container to set. Once cooled to a gel, create a fluid gel by blending it until it is smooth. Pour the fluid gel into a whipping siphon, seal, and charge. You can then dispense when you are ready to use it.

The more iota carrageenan you use the denser the resulting foam will be. The typical range is from 0.2% to 1.0% iota carrageenan by weight. You can also add other stabilizers such as xanthan gum to change the final density of the foam.

Quick Recipe: Chocolate Iota Carrageenan Foam

Combine 400 grams chocolate milk and 2.0 grams iota carrageenan in a pot and blend well. Heat the mixture above 70°C / 158°F or as high as a boil. Remove from the heat, pour into a container and let cool into a gel.

Once the gel has formed, blend it until smooth and pour into a whipping siphon. Charge the siphon and it is ready to dispense. The chocolate foam can be served either hot or cold.

ULTRA-SPERSE FOAMS

Ultra-Sperse is a modified tapioca starch and is used in many of the same ways xanthan gum is used. It is very good at thickening liquids and can be dispersed in hot or cold liquids.

To create foams with Ultra-Sperse, combine it with a liquid and blend to thicken. Pour the thickened liquid into a whipping siphon, seal, and charge.

Ultra-Sperse works with both hot and cold preparations. Typically it is used in ratios of 0.2% to 5%.

Quick Recipe: Piña Colada Foam
With an immersion blender combine 300 grams pineapple juice, 100 grams coconut milk, and 12 grams Ultra-Sperse. Pour into a whipping siphon, seal, and charge. Dispense onto desserts or as a topper for piña coladas.

ULTRA-TEX FOAMS

Ultra-Tex is very similar in use to xanthan gum and Ultra-Sperse. It can thicken liquids at most temperatures and often has a better mouthfeel than xanthan gum does at higher concentrations. It can also be used in gravies and other warm preparations. Usually 1.0-4.0% is used for basic thickening and 4.0-8.0% for major thickening.

Quick Recipe: Gravy Foam

Take 300 grams of good, fresh chicken or beef stock that has been strained and blend 15 grams of Ultra-Tex into it. Pour into a whipping siphon, seal, and charge. Heat to the serving temperature and dispense to serve.

VERSAWHIP FOAMS

Versawhip is a soy protein that is used similarly to egg whites or gelatin in the stabilization of foams, especially whipped ones. It has greater strength than egg whites and a greater temperature range than gelatin. However, Versawhip will not work with products containing fat.

It is also often combined with xanthan gum for more stable foams. Typical ratios are 0.5% to 2.0% for foams with 0.1% to 0.2% xanthan gum added for support. Versawhip is best combined in a standing blender that is running as the powder is sprinkled in. The Versawhip must sit to work well, so refrigerating the mixture for several hours helps to create a more stable foam.

Quick Recipe: Peach Foam

Take 400 grams peach juice or nectar, strained of pulp, and place in a blender. Turn on the blender and form a vortex. Sprinkle in 3 grams Versawhip (0.75%) and 0.8 grams xanthan gum (0.2%) and blend until combined well. Pour into a whipping siphon, seal, and charge. Refrigerate for several hours and then dispense as desired.

XANTHAN GUM FOAMS

Xanthan gum is a very common foam stabilizer. It works by thickening the liquid being foamed which helps to trap the bubbles. Most xanthan gum foams are light and frothy, though xanthan gum is also often used for denser foams in conjunction with another ingredient such as gelatin or agar.

Making a xanthan gum foam is very easy. Simply blend the xanthan gum into the liquid you want to foam. Place the liquid into a whipping siphon, seal, and charge. Xanthan gum foams can be used hot or cold, though they are a little firmer when cold.

For xanthan gum foams, a ratio between 0.2% and 0.8% is typically used. The more xanthan gum you use the denser the foam will be.

Quick Recipe: Raspberry Foam

Combine 400 grams raspberry juice, strained, and 2 grams xanthan gum (0.5%) with a blender until the raspberry juice has thickened. Pour into a whipping siphon, seal, and charge. Dispense as needed.

USES OF FOAMS

I am always adding new techniques to the website. You can follow all the latest techniques I am exploring.

You can find them on our website at:
www.modernistcookingmadeeasy.com/info/
modernist-techniques

There are many, many different uses for foams. I've selected six different categories for this chapter and created several recipes for each one. This should give you a good feel for the different ways foams can be used.

The categories I've picked are:

Savory Sauces
Foams that are typically used as a sauce or garnish on a savory dish.

Aerated Soups
Different soups that can be foamed or aerated to increase the lightness of them.

Dips
Foams often served alongside food that can be dipped in them.

Sweet Foams
Foams that are usually used with sweet dishes and desserts.

Oil Foams
Oil-based foams that are usually used as sauces or dips.

Cocktail and Drink Foams
Foams that are used in drinks and cocktails.

PICKING A USE

Most foams can be used in several different categories. For instance, the Roasted Red Pepper Soup appears in the Aerated Soups section. However, it can also be successfully used as a savory sauce or a dip.

I hope these recipes will inspire you to create and use foams that complement the dishes you are serving.

SAVORY SAUCES

Probably the most popular use of a foam is as a sauce or topping for dishes. Foams for sauces can range from light froths to thick, heavy foams. Almost any ingredient from the Foaming Ingredients chapter can be used, depending on the dish. You can cross-check with the ingredients table to see which ones might work best.

Teriyaki is one of my favorite flavors, whether it is in a stir fry, beef jerky, or used as a marinade. In this recipe I take an easy-to-make teriyaki sauce and turn it into a foam. It's great on meats or vegetables. If you don't feel like making your own teriyaki sauce for the foam you can use a pre-made sauce, just be sure to strain it if it has particles in it.

Tools Needed

Ultra-Sperse
Standing or immersion blender

Ingredients

For the Teriyaki Marinade
⅓ cup soy sauce
¼ cup hoisin sauce
¼ cup brown sugar
½ cup diced pineapple
1 fresh red chile, diced
2 garlic cloves, diced
1 tablespoon grated ginger
3 tablespoons rice vinegar
¾ cup water

For the Foam
400 grams teriyaki marinade
16 grams Ultra-Sperse, 4%

For the Teriyaki Marinade

In the pot combine all of the teriyaki marinade ingredients and bring to a simmer. Gently simmer for 5 minutes and then blend to combine. Remove from the heat and strain.

For the Foam

Blend the teriyaki marinade and Ultra-Sperse together. Pour into your whipping siphon and charge. Heat the whipping siphon in hot water until it is warm, I tend to use water between 55°C / 131°F to 60.5°C / 141°F because that is what my sous vide machine is typically running at but any water below 80°C / 175°F should be fine.

Once the siphon has come up to temperature you can dispense it onto your dishes.

Variation

For a fun party food, you can use agar in place of the Ultra-Sperse and turn the teriyaki sauce into a thick foam that can be used as a dip for steamed vegetables, egg rolls, or chicken skewers. Just add 1% agar to the pot before you bring it to a boil to hydrate it.

I love how flavorful curries can be and this recipe takes advantage of that depth to make a flavorful cream foam. It can be used on many meats or even as a dip for vegetables.

For a lighter foam you can omit the agar and rely on the cream to stabilize the foam.

Tools Needed
Agar
Standing or immersion blender

Ingredients
For the Curry Base
3 tablespoons canola oil
1 onion, chopped
2 carrots, peeled and chopped
1 red bell pepper, chopped
5 garlic cloves, coarsely chopped
2-inch piece fresh ginger, peeled and cut
    into large chunks
2 teaspoons ground coriander
½ teaspoon black pepper
¼-1 teaspoon cayenne pepper, to taste
½ teaspoon garam masala
½ teaspoon ground cloves
500 grams water

For the Foam
300 grams curry base
150 grams heavy cream
3.3 grams agar, 0.75%

For the Curry Base

Heat a pan over medium-high heat with the canola oil in it. Add the onion and cook until it begins to soften, about 5 minutes. Add the carrots and cook for another 5 minutes. Add the red bell pepper and cook for another 5 minutes.

Add the garlic, ginger, coriander, pepper, cayenne, garam masala, and cloves to the pan. Cook for about 10 minutes while stirring occasionally. Add the water and bring to a simmer for about 30 minutes. Strain.

For the Foam

Pour 300 grams curry base into a pot and blend in 3.3 grams agar with an immersion blender. Bring to a boil and let simmer for 3 to 5 minutes. Blend in the cream then remove from the heat, pour into a container, and let it cool.

Once cool, use a standing or immersion blender to blend the gel until smooth. Add to a whipping siphon, seal, and charge. This foam can be used both on hot and cold dishes.

SPICY CHIPOTLE FOAM

This is a simple recipe to put together that results in a smoky, spicy foam. It's a light foam that adds a spicy finish to dishes. I like to use it as a garnish on tacos or quesadillas, or sometimes as a garnish on poached fish.

This recipe can also be adapted to use any hot pepper you like.

Tools Needed
Xanthan gum
Standing or immersion blender

Ingredients
For the Chipotle Puree
100 grams chipotles in adobo sauce
300 grams water or stock

For the Foam
400 grams chipotle puree
1.6 grams xanthan gum, 0.4%

For the Chipotle Puree
Combine the chipotles and water in a pot. Bring to a boil then blend well. Strain the chipotle puree and set aside.

For the Foam
Blend the chipotle puree and xanthan gum together. Pour into a whipping siphon and charge. You can heat the whipping siphon or leave it at room temperature until you are ready to dispense the foam.

JAMAICAN JERK FOAM

Our family started spending Thanksgivings in Jamaica and I've become a huge fan of jerked foods. There are roadside stands everywhere selling jerked chicken, pork, and goat that is just incredible. This is my attempt to take a roadside food and move it into a modernist dish.

If you do not want to make your own jerk paste there are a few good brands available. We always took several bottles of Walkerswood Traditional Jamaican Jerk Seasoning home when we visited and you can now find it in many grocery stores.

Tools Needed

Agar
Standing or immersion blender

Ingredients

For the Jerk Paste
3 to 10 habanero or Scotch bonnet chilies, stemmed and cut in half
1 onion, coarsely chopped
2 bunches scallions (white and green parts), trimmed and coarsely chopped
5 garlic cloves, coarsely chopped
½ cup fresh parsley, coarsely chopped
½ cup fresh cilantro, chopped
2 teaspoons fresh ginger, chopped
2 tablespoons coarse salt
2 tablespoons fresh thyme
1 tablespoon ground allspice
½ teaspoon ground cinnamon
½ teaspoon freshly grated nutmeg
1 teaspoon freshly ground black pepper
¼ cup brown sugar
½ cup fresh lime juice
¼ cup olive oil
2 tablespoons soy sauce
¼ cup cold water, or as needed

For the Jerk Stock
150 grams jerk paste
300 grams stock, usually chicken or vegetable

For the Foam
400 grams jerk stock
2.0 grams agar, 0.5%

For the Jerk Paste

Add all of the dry ingredients to a food processor and process to a paste. Add the remaining liquid ingredients and process until the paste becomes spreadable.

Variation

At this point, you can also use the paste on dishes as a sauce or marinade.

For the Jerk Stock

Combine the jerk paste and stock in a pot and bring to a simmer. Let simmer for 5 minutes and remove from the heat, let cool for 15 minutes so the flavors meld and then strain the stock.

For the Foam

Blend the jerk stock and agar together. Pour into a pot and bring to a boil. Let simmer for 3 to 5 minutes then pour into a container and let it set completely.

Once it is set, cube the gel and puree with a blender until smooth. Add some water if you need to thin it.

Pour the fluid gel into your whipping siphon and charge. Heat the whipping siphon in hot water until it is warm, I tend to use water between 55°C / 131°F to 60.5°C / 141°F because that is what my sous vide machine is typically running at but any water below 80°C / 175°F should be fine.

Once the siphon has come up to temperature you can dispense it onto your dishes.

I live in the New England area and we can get great apple cider from local orchards during most of the year. This cider turns into a fantastic topper for meats, fish, or desserts.

There are many flavor variations you can make just by introducing a small amount of another liquid or some spices. Below are the spices I like to use when I am making pork tenderloin medallions. The bourbon gives it a lot of base flavor and the spices add some high notes for the dish.

Tools Needed
Agar
Xanthan gum
Standing or immersion blender

Ingredients
For the Cider Gel
350 grams apple cider
50 grams bourbon or whisky
3.6 grams agar, 0.9%
1 teaspoon cinnamon
2 teaspoons sweet curry powder
1 teaspoon ground cloves

For the Puree
375 grams cider gel
0.8 grams xanthan gum, 0.2%

For the Cider Gel

Combine all the ingredients except the xanthan gum in a pot and blend together well. Bring to a boil. Let simmer for 3 to 5 minutes then pour into a container and let it set completely.

For the Foam

Cube the gel once it is set then puree it and the xanthan gum with a blender until smooth. Add some water if you need to thin it.

Pour the fluid gel into your whipping siphon and charge. Heat the whipping siphon in hot water until it is warm, I tend to use water between 55°C / 131°F to 60.5°C / 141°F because that is what my sous vide machine is typically running at but any water below 80°C / 175°F should be fine.

Once the siphon has come up to temperature you can dispense it onto your dishes.

Variation

For a nice variation you can turn this into a sweet foam by adding some sugar or honey to it to sweeten it up.

Mango Habanero Froth

This froth adds a spicy, tropical flavor to many dishes. I really like it on soft tacos or as a topper to gazpacho. You can also freeze the foam in molds and use it as a spicy topping on desserts.

The amount of habanero you use will depend on how hot you like your food, and how spicy you want the foam to be. You can also use other juices besides mango, I really like orange or peach juice as well.

If you don't want to make your own mango juice you can find it at many nicer supermarkets or health food stores. You can always use Goya canned juice if you can't find any fresh juice.

Tools Needed
Xanthan gum
Standing or immersion blender

Ingredients
For the Mango-Habanero Infusion
450 grams fresh mango juice
¼-1 habanero, seeds removed and cut in half

For the Foam
400 grams mango-habanero infusion
2.4 grams xanthan gum, 0.6%

For the Mango-Habanero Infusion
Pour the mango juice in a pot and add the habanero pepper. Bring to a boil then simmer for 5 to 10 minutes. Remove the habanero pepper and any seeds.

For the Foam
Blend the mango-habanero infusion and xanthan gum together. Pour into a whipping siphon and charge. You can heat the whipping siphon or leave it at room temperature until you are ready to dispense the foam.

I love how the smokiness of chipotles and bacon go together so well. The cream helps to cut the spiciness and balance out the foam. This chipotle-bacon cream foam is a great topping for beef or pork. It also works very well with potatoes or even as a sauce for vegetables like steamed asparagus.

For a much lighter foam you can omit the agar and just rely on the cream for the foaming.

Tools Needed
Agar
Immersion or standing blender

Ingredients
For the Chipotle-Bacon Cream
200 grams bacon, coarsely diced
300 grams heavy cream
1 to 2 chipotles in adobo sauce

For the foam
300 grams chipotle-bacon cream
2.25 grams agar, 0.75%

For the Chipotle-Bacon Cream

Fry the bacon until it browns and the fat is rendered. Add the cream and chipotles and let simmer for 5 minutes. Let cool for 15 minutes for the flavors to meld. Strain out the bacon and chipotles.

For the Foam

Combine the cream and agar in a pot and blend well. Bring to a simmer. Let simmer for 3 to 5 minutes. Pour into a container and let cool into a gel.

Blend the gel until it is smooth then pour into the whipping siphon then seal and charge the siphon.

You can refrigerate the siphon until you are ready to use it. Before serving, if you have a heat-resistant siphon, you can heat the siphon in a water bath, I've found 38°C / 100°F to 55°C / 131°F works well.

Turn the siphon upside down and dispense directly onto the dish.

AERATED SOUPS

A great use of the whipping siphon is to lighten soups. If you take a soup and foam it using the whipping siphon it will aerate it, adding body and lightness to the soup without diluting the flavors. This works best with bisques and other rich, smooth soups. Lighter, flavorful, and clear soups also respond very well to aeration.

Like all foaming liquids, soups you aerate must be smooth and free of particles. It's best to add any internal or external garnishes after the soup has been foamed. For instance, you could make a clam chowder soup, strain it, then aerate it. The strained solids, such as the bacon, potatoes, and clams, could then be placed in the bottom of the bowl and the soup foamed on top of them. You could also gently stir them in, though this will cause the foam to lose some body.

Many soups will work just fine with no additional stabilizers, especially soups that already have cream in them. You can thicken soups and increase the density of the foam with the addition of xanthan gum, Ultra-Sperse or other thickeners. Stabilizers such as agar or carrageenan can also be added for very thick soups.

Roasted red peppers are a classic Italian offering. Here I use the whipping siphon to aerate them into a light, smooth soup. You can increase or reduce the amount of agar to easily control the thickness of the soup.

I prefer making my own roasted peppers but high-quality store bought ones can be used if you are in a pinch.

In addition to serving it as a soup, this foam can be used in many different ways to turn traditional dishes into modern masterpieces. It's great on fish, asparagus, or even steaks.

Tools Needed
Agar
Standing or immersion blender

Ingredients
For the Roasted Pepper Puree
5-6 red peppers
Olive oil
Salt and pepper
3 cloves garlic, diced
4 sprigs thyme, stems removed
100 grams water or stock

For the Foam
400 grams roasted pepper puree
2.0 grams agar, 0.5%

For the Garnish
Lemon zest
Thyme leaves
Parmesan cheese strips

For the Roasted Pepper Puree

Toss the red peppers with the olive oil then salt and pepper them. Cook them on a grill, or in a hot oven, rotating as needed, until the skins begin to blacken all over.

Remove from the heat. For a more refined presentation the charred skin can be peeled off, though sometimes I like to leave them on since the char adds a nice bitterness to the foam.

Combine the roasted peppers, garlic, thyme, and water in a pot. Bring to a simmer then blend well. Strain the puree and set aside.

For the Foam

Blend the roasted red pepper puree and agar together. Pour into a pot and bring to a boil. Let simmer for 3 to 5 minutes then pour into a container and let it set completely.

Once it is set, cube the gel and puree with a blender until smooth. Add some water if you need to thin it.

Pour the fluid gel into your whipping siphon and charge. Heat the whipper in hot water until it is warm.

Once the siphon has come up to temperature, dispense the foam into bowls. Garnish with the lemon zest, thyme leaves, and parmesan cheese strips.

My mother-in-law always cooks great meals for us when we come to visit. She recently cooked a wonderful sweet potato soup for us that I thought would be great in modernist preparations. I've roasted the sweet potatoes and added some molasses for extra depth of flavor.

The recipe below can also be used for a hearty sauce on meats or vegetables.

Tools Needed
Standing or immersion blender

Ingredients
For the Sweet Potato Soup
3 to 4 sweet potatoes, cut into a large dice
Canola oil
Salt and pepper
200-400 grams chicken stock
1" piece of ginger, peeled and chopped.
10 grams molasses
20 grams thyme leaves
20 grams honey
200 grams heavy cream

For the Garnish
Small marshmallows
Thyme leaves
Walnuts, finely chopped
Molasses

For the Sweet Potato Soup
Preheat an oven to 232°C / 450°F.

Toss the sweet potato chunks with canola oil and salt and pepper. Spread out on a sheet pan and roast until the outsides have browned nicely, typically 20 to 30 minutes.

Place the roasted sweet potatoes into a pot with the chicken stock, ginger, molasses, and thyme. Cook until the sweet potatoes are very soft and the flavors have melded. Start with 200 grams of stock and add more as needed to keep it moist. Add the honey and cream then puree until very smooth using a blender. Strain through a chinois or cheese cloth if you want a finer texture.

For the Foam
Pour the sweet potato soup into your whipping siphon and charge. If desired, heat the whipper in hot water until it is warm.

Dispense the soup into soup bowls or cups. Top the soup with the marshmallows, thyme leaves, and walnuts then finish with a drizzle of molasses.

This is a light and refreshing soup that is great in summer. The watermelon and cucumber complement each other well and the mint and lemon adds hints of brightness and nice background flavors.

Tools Needed
Gelatin
Standing or immersion blender

Ingredients
For the Soup
300 grams watermelon, peeled and deseeded
100 grams cucumber, peeled and deseeded
Juice of ½ lemon
10 to 20 mint leaves
Salt and pepper

For the Foam
400 grams cucumber-watermelon soup
1 gelatin sheet or ¼ packet, 0.45%

For the Garnish
Mint leaves
Lemon zest or strips
Crumbled blue cheese
Cherry tomatoes, halved

For the Soup

Combine all the ingredients and blend until smooth. Taste for seasoning and add more mint or lemon juice as needed. Strain through a chinois or cheese cloth.

For the Foam

Place the cucumber-watermelon soup into a pot.

For sheet gelatin, bloom the gelatin in a bowl of cold water for 5 to 10 minutes, gently wring out the water, then add to the soup. For powdered gelatin, add directly to the soup and let it bloom for 5 to 10 minutes.

Once bloomed, heat the pot over medium heat while stirring until the gelatin dissolves.

Pour the cucumber-watermelon soup into a whipping siphon and charge. Refrigerate for several hours, at least 2 to 3, until the gelatin sets.

Once set, dispense the soup into soup bowls or cups. Top with the mint leaves, lemon zest, blue cheese, and cherry tomatoes.

DIPS

Foams can also be used very effectively as dips. Lights foams and froths make good dipping sauces while heavier foams can result in hearty, creamy dips. Almost any flavorful liquid can be turned into a dip.

Buffalo Sauce Dip

Spicy, crispy Buffalo wings are a favorite snack of mine. This recipe combines a traditional Buffalo sauce with chicken stock which is then foamed to create a great dip for vegetables. The foam can also be used on wraps or even tacos.

Franks is the traditional hot sauce used in Buffalo sauces but any cayenne-based hot sauce will do.

Tools Needed
Agar
Mono and diglyceride flakes
Standing or immersion blender

Ingredients
150 grams hot sauce
75 grams chicken stock
25 grams vinegar
15 grams Worcestershire sauce
2.5 grams agar, 1%
150 grams butter
11.5 grams mono and diglyceride (glycerin) flakes, 5.0%

Blend the hot sauce, chicken stock, vinegar, Worcestershire sauce, and agar together. Pour into a pot and bring to a boil. Let simmer for 3 to 5 minutes then pour into a container and let it set completely.

Once it is set, cube the gel and puree with a blender until smooth.

Melt the butter in a pot on medium heat. Add the glycerin flakes and stir until they have melted and are mixed evenly into the butter.

While blending, slowly pour the butter mixture into the hot sauce mixture. Blend until combined.

Pour the mixture into the whipping siphon, seal it, and charge. When you are ready to serve it, dispense the foam into a bowl for dipping. The colder the foam becomes the thicker it gets. The foam is also great as a garnish for chicken or fish.

CREAMY SOUTHWESTERN BLACK BEAN DIP

This black bean foam is rich and creamy due to the addition of the cream cheese. It can be used in place of beans on many dishes or as a fancy dip for chips or vegetables.

Tools Needed
Standing blender or food processor

Ingredients
For the Bean Puree
40 grams canola oil
½ onion, coarsely chopped
5 garlic cloves, coarsely chopped
1 teaspoon coriander
1 teaspoon cumin
1 teaspoon paprika
Salt and pepper
300 grams black beans, cooked
150 grams chicken stock
20 grams lime juice
Hot sauce to taste

For the Foam
350 grams bean puree
100 grams cream cheese

For the Bean Puree
Heat a pan over medium to medium-high heat. Add the oil, onion, garlic, and spices and sauté until the onion is translucent. Add the remaining ingredients and bring to a simmer. Adjust for seasonings and let simmer for five to 10 minutes. Remove from the heat and let cool slightly.

Pour into a blender or food processor and process until very smooth. For a finer consistency you can strain the puree.

For the Foam
Combine the bean puree and cream cheese and mix or blend until fully combined. Pour into a whipping siphon and charge.

When you are ready to serve it, dispense the foam into a bowl for dipping.

Spinach dips are very popular at many restaurants. I like to take a classic creamed spinach and turn it into a foam for dipping. It can be served with roasted pita squares or even just vegetables and chips. You can also use this dip as a sauce for steak or chicken.

Tools Needed
Standing blender or food processor
Xanthan gum, optional

Ingredients
For the Spinach Puree
30 grams butter
½ onion, coarsely diced
10 garlic cloves, minced
2 grams cayenne powder
600 grams spinach
2 grams ground nutmeg
1 gram ground clove
300 grams heavy cream
Salt and pepper

For the Foam
400 grams spinach puree
0.4-1.6 grams xanthan gum, optional, 0.1% - 0.4%

For the Spinach Puree
Heat a pan over medium to medium-high heat. Add the butter and melt. Add the onion, garlic, and cayenne powder and sauté until the onion is translucent. Add the remaining ingredients and bring to a simmer. Adjust for seasonings and let simmer for five minutes. Remove from the heat and let cool slightly.

Pour into a blender or food processor and process until very smooth, then strain.

For the Foam
If the spinach needs thickening you can blend in some xanthan gum. Pour the spinach puree into a whipping siphon and charge.

When you are ready to serve it, dispense the foam into a bowl for dipping.

SWEET FOAMS

Sweet foams are usually used as dessert toppings, or even desserts in and of themselves. They are typically sweetened through the addition of sugar or honey, or often times with fruit juices or purees.

This section highlights several different uses for sweet foams including simple sauces, airy meringues, and even microwaved sponge cakes.

Maple-Pecan Milk Foam

I love the flavor pairing of pecans and maple. For this recipe I make a pecan infused milk that I add maple syrup to and then foam. It's fantastic on silver dollar pancakes, shortcakes, or as a topping for sliced bananas.

The maple-pecan milk takes some time to make but most of it is just the mixture soaking in the refrigerator. The longer you soak the mixture the stronger the flavor of the milk will be.

You can easily increase or reduce the amount of agar to change the consistency of the foam to meets the needs of your meal.

Tools Needed
Agar
Standing or immersion blender

Ingredients
For the Maple-Pecan Milk
150 grams pecans
30 grams canola oil
300 grams milk
75 grams maple syrup

For the Foam
400 grams maple-pecan milk
3.0 grams agar, 0.75%

For the Maple-Pecan Milk
Heat an oven to 176ºC / 350ºF . Toss the pecans with the canola oil and spread out on a sheet pan. Bake for 5 to 10 minutes.

Combine the roasted pecans and the milk in a pot and bring to a simmer. Stir in the maple syrup and remove from the heat. Blend the mixture very well and refrigerate for at least 12 hours and up to a few days.

Remove the mixture from the refrigerator and blend a final time. Strain to remove any pieces of the nuts.

For the Foam
Blend the maple-pecan milk and agar together. Pour into a pot and bring to a boil. Let simmer for 3 to 5 minutes then pour into a container and let it set completely.

Once it is set, cube the gel and puree with a blender until smooth. Add some water or milk if you need to thin it.

Pour the fluid gel into your whipping siphon and charge. You can now dispense the foam as needed.

Variation
I'll often make extra maple-pecan milk and create a savory version of the foam. I'll add some chipotle powder or curry powder when I add the agar. The resulting foam can be used as a great topping for pork or lamb.

FROZEN BLUEBERRY FOAM

Another way to utilize foams is to freeze them. The color and flavor of blueberries holds up well to being frozen. The frozen foam goes great with different desserts like cake or ice cream. I even use it as a garnish on drinks such as lemonade or blueberry mojitos. The frozen foams can be delicate so I prefer to freeze them in flexible silicon molds so they are easier to unmold.

You can make frozen foams out of most flavorful foams. Just dispense the foam into the molds and then place in a freezer or blast chiller. After the foams have set you can unmold and serve them.

If you can't find blueberry juice you can puree blueberries with some water or orange juice and then strain the liquid.

Tools Needed
Gelatin
Silicon molds

Ingredients
400 grams fresh blueberry juice
2 gelatin sheets or ½ packet, 0.9%

Place the blueberry juice into a pot.

For sheet gelatin, bloom the gelatin in a bowl of cold water for 5 to 10 minutes, gently wring out the water, then add to the juice. For powdered gelatin, add directly to the juice and let it bloom for 5 to 10 minutes.

Once bloomed, heat the pot over medium heat while stirring until the gelatin dissolves.

Pour the blueberry mixture into a whipping siphon and charge. Refrigerate for several hours, at least 2 to 3, until the gelatin sets.

Dispense the foam into the silicon molds and place in the freezer. Once the foam is set and fully frozen, unmold and serve it.

PEACH DESSERT FOAM

During summer the peaches are soft, sweet, and completely delicious. I'm always trying to find new ways to get them into my cooking. This peach dessert foam showcases the flavor of the peaches while still being an upscale dish.

I like to serve it in small individual bowls garnished with some mint leaves, orange zest, and a few peach slices. It can also be used as a fun twist for strawberry shortcake or even just on some brownies or chocolate chip cookies.

Tools Needed
Gelatin
Standing or immersion blender

Ingredients
For the Peach Puree
400 grams fresh peach chunks
50 grams orange juice
21 grams molasses
10 grams mint leaves

For the Foam
2 gelatin sheets or ½ packet of gelatin (0.9%)
400 grams peach puree

For the Garnish
Mint leaves
Orange zest
Peach slices

For the Peach Puree
Combine all the peach puree ingredients and blend until smooth. The puree should still be a little runny. If it is too dense add more orange juice or water to thin it out. Strain out any solids.

For the Foam
Add the peach puree to a pot.

For sheet gelatin, bloom the gelatin in a bowl of cold water for 5 to 10 minutes, gently wring out the water, then add to the puree. For powdered gelatin, add directly to the puree and let it bloom for 5 to 10 minutes.

Once bloomed, heat the pot over medium heat while stirring until the gelatin dissolves.

Remove from the heat then pour the peach mixture into a whipping siphon, charge, and shake several times. Refrigerate for several hours, at least 2 to 3, until the gelatin sets. The foam will now be ready to dispense.

To serve, dispense the peach foam into individual dishes. Garnish with the mint leaves, orange zest, and peach slices then serve.

DARK CHOCOLATE MOUSSE

There is nothing like a rich, dark chocolate mousse to finish off a great dinner. Turning the mousse into a foam helps lighten it while also adding some versatility to how it can be served. I like to serve this mousse by itself with some shaved chocolate and mint leaves. It can also be used as a decadent topping for many different desserts.

This is a basic mousse recipe to show how easy it can be but feel free to expand on it. Replacing some of the cream with Grand Marnier adds a nice orange flavor to it. You can stir in some chile pepper powder for a spicy. This same recipe also works well with milk chocolate or a combination of light and dark. You can also lighten it up by adding more cream to the mixture.

The quality of chocolate you use will greatly affect the end flavor of the mousse. The mousse should be dispensed warm or the chocolate can solidify.

Ingredients

300 grams chocolate, chopped into chunks
150 grams whipping cream

Place all the ingredients into a pot set over low to medium-low heat. Heat the mixture gently while stirring occasionally until the chocolate is fully melted and combined with the cream. Try to keep the cream below a simmer. You can also use a double boiler or sous vide machine to melt the chocolate.

Remove from the heat and pour the chocolate mixture into a whipping siphon, charge, and shake several times. The foam will now be ready to dispense and should be dispensed warm or it can solidify.

LEMON MERINGUES

Lemon meringues are a classic sweet. Here we take the typically sweet but bland filling and add all the flavors from a lemon meringue pie to turn it into a flavorful and versatile foam.

It can be used for a topping on pie or even on cakes and brownies. You can also bake the meringues at 150°C / 300°F to 175°C / 350°F for one to two hours or place them in a dehydrator to dry them out for a crispy snack. Occasionally egg foams will not set properly when hot. In this case you can cool them in the refrigerator until they set and then re-heat them.

For numerous variations, you can replace the lemon extract with other flavored extracts or essential oils.

Tools Needed
Standing or immersion blender
Sous vide bath

Ingredients
200 grams egg whites
100 grams sugar, preferably superfine
2.5 grams cream of tartar
6 grams lemon extract

Blend the egg whites, sugar, and cream of tartar together then place in a sous vide bag and seal. Cook for 35 minutes in a 75°C / 167°F water bath. If you don't have a sous vide machine you can fill a small cooler with the 75°C / 167°F water or keep it that temperature in a large pot of water on the stove.

Remove from the bag and blend with 6 grams lemon extract until smooth. Strain into a whipping siphon, seal, and charge.

You can heat the siphon as long as you do not go above the initial cooking temperature and you have a heat resistant whipping siphon.

Dispense to serve.

MICROWAVE SPONGE CAKE

One of the more interesting uses for whipping siphons is to make microwave sponge cakes. Many of the modernist chefs have shared their recipes but the actual execution is typically the same and is very simple.

Make your favorite cake batter, even if it's out of a box, then charge it in the whipping siphon. Dispense into a paper cup and microwave for 45 to 70 seconds. You always make one cup at a time, which also gives you the opportunity to narrow down the time you need to microwave it.

Most all-paper cups will work and paper coffee cups work well since they are designed to handle heat.

Tools Needed
Microwaveable paper cups

Ingredients
400 grams prepared cake batter

Pour the batter into a whipping siphon, charge, and shake several times. Cut a few vertical slits into the bottom sides of a paper cup, these will let the steam escape. Fill the cup ¼ to ½ full with the siphoned batter.

Place the cup in the microwave and heat for 45 to 70 seconds, depending on the cup size and batter used. Remove from the microwave and let cool for a few seconds. Turn the cup upside down, remove the cake, and serve.

OIL FOAMS

Oil foams are a great way to incorporate oils and fats into your dishes while avoiding the fatty pools that can occur. The processes of foaming also makes oil go a longer way, keeping dishes lighter than they would be otherwise.

Most oil foams make use of mono and diglyceride flakes, also known as glycerin flakes, to thicken the oil and stabilize the foam. Any type of oil or fat can be used and it is often flavored ahead of time either through infusing or steeping spices and herbs in the oil before foaming it. Most oil foams hold up well to heat but the colder the foam becomes the thicker it gets.

This chile spread infuses the heat, smokiness and flavor of dried chiles into canola oil which is then thickened into a foam. It is a good topping for grilled meat or a spicy spread for fresh bread. This process of infusing oil with flavors before thickening it leads to countless variations you can adapt to any dish.

You can use any chile peppers you prefer. I really enjoy ancho peppers for a fruity flavor, chipotle for a more smokey flavor, or for more spice something like an arbol, Tien Tsin, or cayenne pepper.

Tools Needed
Mono and Diglyceride (Glycerin) Flakes
Standing or immersion blender, optional

Ingredients
For the Chile Oil
300 grams canola oil
2-4 dried chile peppers, coarsely chopped
¼ onion, coarsely chopped
3 cloves garlic, coarsely chopped
Salt and pepper

For the Foam
300 grams chile oil
15 grams mono and diglyceride (glycerin) flakes, 5.0%

For the Chile Oil
Combine the canola oil, chile peppers, onion, and garlic in a pot set over medium heat. Salt and pepper them. Heat for 15 minutes, until the onions soften.

If you want a more flavorful oil you can now puree with a blender.

Strain the canola oil to remove the solids.

For the Foam
Return the oil to the pot and place back on medium heat. Add the glycerin flakes and stir until they have melted. Remove the pot from the heat and carefully pour into a heat resistant whipping siphon. If you prefer, you can let the oil cool to room temperature before pouring.

Refrigerate the whipping siphon for several hours. Once cold, dispense the oil from the whipping siphon.

PESTO FOAM

Pesto is a classic Italian condiment that goes great with anything from pasta to meat to fish. In this recipe I infuse olive oil with the flavors of pesto and then turn it into a foam.

This process works well for many different types of oil and nut-based sauces.

Tools Needed
Mono and Diglyceride (Glycerin) Flakes

Ingredients
For the Pesto Oil
300 grams olive oil
75 grams basil
125 grams pine nuts
3 cloves garlic, coarsely chopped

For the Foam
300 grams pesto oil
22 grams mono and diglyceride (glycerin)
    flakes, 7.5%

For the Pesto Oil
Preheat the oven to 121°C / 250°F.

Combine the olive oil, basil, pine nuts, and garlic in a pan. Place in the oven for 30 to 60 minutes, stirring occasionally, until the oil is fragrant and takes on the flavor of the pesto.

Strain the olive oil to remove the solids.

For the Foam
Place the oil in a pot and place on medium heat. Add the glycerin flakes and stir until they have melted. Remove the pot from the heat and carefully pour into a heat resistant whipping siphon. If you prefer, you can let the oil cool to room temperature before pouring.

Refrigerate the whipping siphon for several hours. Once cold, you can dispense the oil from the whipping siphon.

BROWNED BUTTER FOAM

*The process of browning butter adds a great
nutty flavor to the butter. It's often used as a
base for many different sauces or as a flavorful
cooking oil. Here, I turn it into a thick foam that
can be used as a sauce or topping for many
dishes. It goes great on top of a steak or grilled
chicken. I also really like it as a spread for
muffins, corn bread, or biscuits.*

Tools Needed
Mono and Diglyceride (Glycerin) Flakes

Ingredients
300 grams butter, cut into chunks
22 grams mono and diglyceride (glycerin)
  flakes, 7.5%

Place a pot over medium heat. Place the
butter into the pot and lightly whisk it
as it melts. The butter will begin to
foam. As the foam settles, the milk solids
will start to brown. Once the butter
begins to brown and smell nutty, remove
it from the heat. The butter can very
quickly go from browned to burned so
keep an eye on it.

Add the glycerin flakes and stir until
they have melted. If they don't melt
completely you can put the pot back on
the heat until they do. Strain the oil and
carefully pour into a heat resistant
whipping siphon. If you prefer, you can
let the oil cool to room temperature
before pouring.

Refrigerate the whipping siphon for
several hours. Once cold, you can
dispense the oil from the whipping
siphon.

COCKTAIL AND DRINK FOAMS

There are several ways to use foams in cocktails and drinks. One is to foam a specific ingredient which can then be added to the remaining ingredients for the drink. For instance, you could create strawberry lemonade by making a normal lemonade mixture and then topping it with a strawberry foam.

Another use of foams in drinks is to add texture and body to a drink via a froth. For example, you could make a light froth with orange juice to serve at brunch as a way to lighten up the traditional breakfast drink.

A third way is to fully transform the cocktail or drink into a foam and serve it in a modernist style. You could make a mojito mix, turn it into a dense foam, and serve it in a small glass with a spoon. This method also works very well with milk based drinks, which are easy to turn into mousse-like foams.

ORANGE JUICE FROTH

I like to serve this orange juice froth as a drink during breakfast or brunch. It uses just a little xanthan gum to thicken it and some lecithin to hold it together. It is still a very wet, refreshing drink.

I often like the addition of some cinnamon and a mint leaf or two but it is very good served straight up as well.

Tools Needed
Xanthan gum
Immersion blender
Lecithin

Ingredients
400 grams orange juice, preferably fresh
0.8 grams lecithin, 0.2%
0.8 grams xanthan gum, 0.2%

Strain the orange juice if it has pulp.

Combine the orange juice, xanthan gum, and lecithin then blend well. Pour into a whipping siphon, seal, and charge.

Dispense into a small cup and serve.

I love a good sangria during summer. The fruit juices complement the wine perfectly and it's so refreshing, especially when you add some club soda to lighten it up. This recipe is for a fancier version of sangria I like to serve at parties. I create a sangria foam which is dispensed into a glass of club soda. It's a wonderful, invigorating drink that people just love.

I prefer to use orange juice and grape juice in my sangria but you can use any fruit juice or additional alcohol you like.

Tools Needed
Xanthan gum
Versawhip
Immersion or standing blender

Ingredients
For the Sangria Foam
260 grams chianti
50 grams sugar, preferably powdered or
    superfine
70 grams orange juice, pulp-free or strained
70 grams grape juice
1 gram xanthan gum, 0.25%
2 grams versawhip, 0.5%

For the Drink
Club soda
Fruit or berries
Mint leaves
Lemon or lime wedges

For the Foam
Combine all the sangria foam ingredients and blend well. Pour into a whipping siphon, seal, and charge.

To serve, fill a glass with ice and fill half way with club soda. Shake the siphon several times then turn it upside down and dispense directly into the glass, filling the glass most of the way to the top. Top with some fruit, the mint leaves, and citrus wedges.

Party Tip
If you need to make lots of sangria for a larger party, or a "thirsty" group, you can scale the recipe up and make it in a large pitcher. Just combine the foam ingredients in the pitcher and blend well with an immersion blender then store it in the refrigerator. Then you can quickly refill the whipping siphon from the pitcher whenever it runs out.

BLUEBERRY LEMONADE

This is a refreshing take on blueberry lemonade that will have your guests talking. It is a light blueberry froth dispensed on top of a glass of lemonade. The blueberry foam slowly filters into the drink, changing the flavor of the lemonade the longer you drink it. It is a quick recipe to make and is a great way to elevate a common drink.

If you can't find blueberry puree or blueberry juice, it is easy to make your own. In a blender, combine blueberries with some water or orange juice and puree until it becomes very smooth. Simply strain the puree to remove pieces of blueberries and the puree is ready to use.

Tools Needed
Xanthan gum
Immersion or standing blender

Ingredients
For the Foam
400 grams blueberry puree or blueberry
   juice, strained
1 gram xanthan gum, 0.25%

For the Drink
Lemonade
Blueberries
Mint leaves

Combine the blueberry puree and xanthan gum then blend well. Pour into a whipping siphon, seal, and charge.

To serve, add ice to a glass and fill most of the way with lemonade. Shake the siphon several times then turn it upside down and dispense directly into the glass, filling the glass most of the way to the top. Top with some blueberries and mint leaves.

WHITE RUSSIAN AMUSE BOUCHE

I always enjoy white Russians, there's something about the combination of cream, Kahlua, and vodka that is refreshing. It's sweet without being cloying and the cream is nice and rich. It also always reminds me of the Big Lebowski.

I like to make this White Russian foam and present it as an amuse bouche before serving dessert, or as a small dessert on its own after a big meal. Of course, you can also use the foam as a wonderful topping for brownies or ice cream. Even the Dude would abide.

Tools Needed
Immersion blender
Gelatin

Ingredients
For the White Russian
90 grams cream
2 gelatin sheets or ½ packet, 1.2%
150 grams vodka
60 grams Kahlua

Place the cream into a pot.

For sheet gelatin, bloom the gelatin in a bowl of cold water for 5 to 10 minutes, gently wring out the water, then add to the cream. For powdered gelatin, add directly to the cream and let it bloom for 5 to 10 minutes.

Once bloomed, heat the pot over medium heat while stirring until the gelatin dissolves.

Blend in the vodka and Kahlua then pour the mixture into a whipping siphon and charge. Refrigerate for several hours, at least 2 to 3, until the gelatin sets.

SECTION THREE

INFUSING

Infusions have long been a part of various cuisines and cooking methods. From classic drinks like Limoncello to flavored oils and fruity vinegars, infusions have been used extensively in cooking. When done in the traditional manner, the infusion process takes anywhere from a few hours to several months. Using a whipping siphon for infusions speeds the process up and cuts the infusion time to just a couple of minutes.

Whipping siphon infusions were popularized by Dave Arnold from the French Culinary Institute. The process, similar to the process for nitrogen cavitation, uses the pressure generated in the whipping siphon to flavor the liquids. The pressure causes the penetration of the N2O into the flavoring agents. Once the pressure is released, the gas rushes out, carrying flavor compounds into the liquid and infusing it with flavor. The whole process only takes a minute or two, making it a very effective way to flavor liquids.

The whipping siphon infusion process can't replace some traditional infusions but it is a technique worth experimenting with. These infusions are also a wonderful way to create flavored liquids for different foams.

THE INFUSING PROCESS

The infusion process is about the same for any liquid you want to flavor. Pick your flavoring agents, usually spices, herbs, or other flavorful items. Clean the flavoring agents and place them into the whipping siphon. There are many variables that determine how much to use, but a good rule of thumb is 10 to 45 grams of flavoring agents for every 250 grams of liquid.

Make sure your liquid is warm, this will speed up the infusion process, and pour it over the flavoring agents in the siphon. Seal the siphon and charge. Typically, a 1-pint siphon will need 1 charge and a 1-quart siphon will need 2.

Briefly swirl the siphon around and then let it sit under pressure. The longer the infusion sits the stronger it will be. Most infusions are best after 30 seconds to 3 minutes.

Vent the siphon and strain out the liquid. Many liquids taste better if they are left to sit for 5 to 10 minutes after they have been strained.

FLAVORING INFUSIONS

By combining different flavoring agents and liquids you can create an unlimited number of infusions. Here are some guidelines for creating your own infusions.

Amount of Flavoring Agent

There are no hard and fast numbers for the amount of flavoring agent to use in infusions, especially since you can use almost anything as a flavoring agent. However, most infusions use between 10 and 45 grams of flavoring agents for every 250 grams of liquid. The amount of flavoring agent used depends on several factors.

Desired Strength of Infusion

The first variable that will determine how much flavoring agent to use is how strong you want the resulting infusion to be. If you are trying to add subtle background hints to a liquid you will want to use less flavoring agents than if you are trying to create a bold liquid that tastes strongly of the flavoring agents.

Strength of the Liquid Being Flavored

The base taste of the liquid you are flavoring makes a big difference in how much flavoring agent you need. If you are trying to add flavor to a neutral spirit like vodka you can use less flavoring agents than if you are flavoring a full-flavored liquid like dark rum, olive oil, or maple syrup.

Strength of Flavoring Agents

Some flavoring agents are much more potent than others. If you are using basil or coriander in your infusion you will need more than if you are infusing chile peppers or rosemary.

Types of Flavoring Agents

There are many different types of flavoring agents people have used to make successful infusions.

Herbs and Spices

Herbs and spices are classic flavoring agents that work great for infusions. Many of the flavors of herbs and spices readily transfer to the liquid during the infusion process. They are great for making the flavored oils I love to use on bread or pastas. Many flavor combinations are also excellent for alcohols and you can make some very creative flavored cocktails.

I've done successful infusions with fresh and dried mint, basil, thai basil, oregano, star anise, cinnamon, coriander, dried chiles, and many others. Dried spices can also be toasted for additional flavor.

If you want to maintain a clear infusion when using herbs, do not crush them unless you are using the infusion immediately or the liquid is dark. Infusions made from crushed herbs can quickly turn brown.

Fruits, Vegetables, and Berries

You can also get a lot of flavor out of fruits, vegetables, and berries. Raspberries and strawberries are great in vinegars and alcohols. Chile peppers create fruity and spicy infusions. Vegetables like bell peppers and cucumbers create more subtle infusions. Carrots do not seem to infuse well, as the bitter flavors are stronger in the infusion than the sweet flavors.

The zest of citrus like lemon, lime, and orange is another great way to add flavors. When using zest be sure to avoid as much of the pith as possible because the bitter flavors it contains are readily transferred during the infusing process.

Other Ingredients

Almost anything can be used as a flavoring agent. The Modernist Cuisine team uses crushed candy canes to make a Candy Cane Vodka.

You can make smoky infusions by pumping smoke into the siphon or through the addition of charred wood chips. Different edible flowers can create floral infusions.

Some people cold "roast" coffee with 5 to 10 minutes of infusion time. Teas are also easily cold "brewed" using the infusion process.

The French Culinary Institute mentions using cocoa nibs for a chocolaty infusion. You can even make meat infusions by using bacon, chicken, smoked salmon, or other cooked meats as your flavoring agent.

Types of Liquids

You can infuse just about any type of liquid using a whipping siphon.

Alcohols

One of the most popular liquids to infuse is alcohol. The infusions range from subtly flavoring vodkas to creating bold, spiced rums, and even making homemade bitters or liqueurs. It's a great way to alter the flavors of a spirit or create your own strongly flavored spirits.

Alcohol infusions are often used as a component in a cocktail or as a stand alone sipping drink. Also, because of the small amounts of alcohol needed for infusions, typically 4 to 8 ounces / 120 to 240 milliliters, you can quickly make many specialty infusions that would usually take days or weeks and require bottles of alcohol using traditional methods.

A good rule of thumb for alcohol infusions is 8 fluid oz / 240 ml liquor to 10 to 15 grams dried spices or ⅓ cup chopped fruit or berries.

Vinegars

Flavored vinegars are a great way to add splashes of flavor to salads, vinaigrettes, meat, or fish. There are many varieties of flavored vinegars you can purchase but most of them are very expensive compared to making them yourself. Making your own vinegar infusions is an inexpensive way to get a lot of flavor into your vinegars and to precisely control its flavor profile.

Herbed vinegars like tarragon, rosemary, or thyme are really good. Fruity vinegars using raspberries, peaches, strawberries, and other fruits or berries are also very tasty.

Oils

Creating oil infusions is an excellent way to add flavor to your favorite oils. They are wonderful as part of a vinaigrette, drizzled on fresh breads or pasta, or even as a topper for vegetables. Some typical oil infusions are woody herbs like rosemary and thyme oil, chile pepper oil, or even citrus oils like lemon.

When making oil infusions, be sure to thoroughly clean the flavoring agents before using them. The infusion process doesn't have any effect on bacteria that may be present so there is always the same risk of botulism you have with traditional oil infusions.

Water

While water might not seem as exciting as the other liquids, it is great when all you want is to extract the pure flavors of the flavoring agents. Water-based infusions are similar to microstocks in many ways and can be pure extracts of flavors.

The water infusions can be made of any flavoring agent. Once the infusion has been made you can use it as part of a sauce, in a cocktail, or even transform it using modernist techniques into a foam or gel.

Other Liquids

People have experimented with many different liquids for infusions. Modernist Cuisine discusses infusing maple syrup with aged whiskey barrel chips.

Simple syrups can easily be infused. This can be useful for many cocktails, such as making a mint simple syrup for mojitos, or orange peel simple syrup for Old Fashioneds.

Other already flavored liquids can be infused as well. Fruit or vegetable juices can have other flavors infused into them. Tea or coffee can also be infused with new flavors.

Ideas in Food has also experimented with infusing porous solids, such as mozzarella cheese, using this method.

Infusing Tips and Tricks

Here are some of my tips and tricks to help you successfully create infusions using your whipping siphon.

Use Warm Liquids

When using a whipping siphon to make infusions, try to use warm liquids whenever you can. Warm liquids work more quickly and make stronger infusions than cold liquids. The liquid doesn't have to be hot, just room temperature or slightly warmer. Once the infusion has been made you can chill the liquid back down before serving it.

Flavors Move At Different Rates

The flavors that get pulled out during the infusing process move at different rates. An infusion made for five minutes is not only stronger than a one minute infusion, it will have a different flavor profile.

This is similar to brewing tea. The most subtle and volatile flavors are pulled out of the tea very quickly. The longer the tea steeps the more bitter the tea becomes as the less volatile bitter flavors slowly get pulled out.

Don't Overfill

As in most techniques using the whipping siphon, you want to be sure not to go above the fill line on the siphon. Overfilling can make it hard to vent the siphon without spraying the infusion out the nozzle.

Let it Stand

Many infusions, especially ones made using alcohol or water, benefit greatly by sitting for 5 to 10 minutes after the infusion has been strained. This settling process gives the flavors time to fully develop and stand out in the infusion.

For Clear Infusions

If you want to keep an infusion clear there are a few tricks. Blanche any herbs in boiling water for 30 to 60 seconds to lock in the colors. This process will help prevent the color from leeching out into the infusion.

Try to use whole herbs or larger pieces of herbs. Cutting or crushing herbs that go into the infusion can turn it brown.

More Surface Area for Faster Infusions

The more surface area your flavoring agents have the faster their flavors are absorbed. This is especially true of fruits and vegetables, or other larger flavoring agents.

Venting Speed Doesn't Matter

There is some disagreement on this tip but most people seem to agree that the speed you vent the siphon doesn't dramatically affect the flavor of the infusion. However, venting the siphon quickly can more easily lead to shooting the infusion out the nozzle. Because of this, I tend to always vent it slowly.

Don't Skimp on Quality

Remember that infusions are like any other kind of cooking and the quality of ingredients you put into them will greatly affect the quality of the result. Using cheap alcohol or oils will result in less flavorful infusions. While you don't always have to use top of the line ingredients, you should definitely use something of good quality. I only use something in my infusions if I would be fine using it alone.

Strain for Clarity

For more clarity in your infusions you should usually strain out the flavoring agents. For larger ingredients a normal strainer will work fine. For smaller ingredients, especially ones that break into particles, you can use a chinois, cheesecloth, or even coffee filters.

INFUSING ALCOHOLS

There are many ways to flavor alcohols, from lightly flavored vodkas to heavier spiced drinks and bitters. This section showcases a few different types of alcohol infusions to provide a basis for your experiments to launch from.

Bourbon is by far my favorite alcohol and I'm always looking for new ways to try it. This recipe adds some great citrus notes from the orange peel and spicy sharpness from the cinnamon. I prefer to use Bulleit Bourbon for this infusion but any decent bourbon or rye you have on hand will work well.

This infusion is great on the rocks or as the base bourbon in an Old Fashioned or Manhattan.

Ingredients
230 grams bourbon
1 cinnamon stick
2 oranges

Make sure the bourbon is at least room temperature or slightly warmer. Wash and dry the cinnamon and oranges. Zest the oranges, either fine or in strips, being careful to remove any pith. Put the orange zest and cinnamon into the whipping siphon. Pour the bourbon into the whipping siphon.

Seal the whipping siphon, charge it, and swirl for 20 to 30 seconds. Let the siphon sit for 1 minute longer. Place a towel over the top of the siphon and slowly vent it.

Strain the orange-cinnamon bourbon and let sit for at least 5 minutes before using.

LIME-JALAPEÑO TEQUILA

This lime-jalapeño tequila infusion adds great spiciness to a margarita, Tequila Sunrise, or even in a Bloody Mary in place of the vodka. The infusion also goes really well with fruit juices and club soda for refreshing summer drinks.

Ingredients
230 grams tequila
2 jalapeño peppers, coarsely chopped
2 limes

Make sure the tequila is at least room temperature or slightly warmer. Wash and dry the jalapeño peppers and limes. Zest the limes, either fine or in strips, being careful to remove any pith. Put the jalapeño peppers and lime zest into the whipping siphon. Pour the tequila into the whipping siphon.

Seal the whipping siphon, charge it, and swirl for 20 to 30 seconds. Let the siphon sit for 1 minute longer. Place a towel over the top of the siphon and slowly vent it.

Strain the lime-jalapeño tequila and let sit for at least 5 minutes before using.

BLUEBERRY VODKA

I love blueberries and the vodka readily takes up their flavors. I like to drink this chilled in a martini glass or with club soda and lime for a nice spritzer. The blueberry flavor is subtle but it still adds a nice fruity undertone to the vodka.

You can follow this recipe with many different types of fruits. Berries tend to work great and raspberry or blackberry vodka turns out really well.

Ingredients
230 grams vodka
90 grams blueberries, smashed

Make sure the vodka is at least room temperature or slightly warmer. Wash and dry the blueberries then put them into the whipping siphon. Pour the vodka into the whipping siphon over the blueberries.

Seal the whipping siphon, charge it, and swirl for 20 to 30 seconds. Let the siphon sit for 1 minute longer. Place a towel over the top of the siphon and slowly vent it.

Strain the blueberry vodka and let sit for at least 5 minutes before using.

INFUSING OILS

Infused oils are a great way to subtly add flavors to dishes. Oils can be lightly flavored, only adding background notes, or they can be full of flavors and be the highlight of a dish.

There are many uses for infused oils once you have created them. They can be used as finishing oils, drizzled over hot foods right before serving. They can be used as dipping oils for breads or vegetables. For more dramatic presentations they can be turned into foams or spreads using the whipping siphon.

HERB-INFUSED OLIVE OIL

The herbs in this olive oil give it a great, deep flavor. The oil is wonderful drizzled on fish or used as a dip for fresh bread. I used these herbs because I usually have them in my garden but you can use any you have on hand.

This recipe is designed to showcase how easy it is to make infused oils. If you want a specific flavor profile you can use any set of herbs you like. Other spices also work well, like cinnamon, star anise, or coriander.

You can also infuse different oils. Canola is nice and neutral, so takes on flavors easily. Olive oil has a rich, deep flavor and holds up well to strong spices. Peanut or sesame oil can be used for Asian blends.

Ingredients
225 grams olive oil
5 grams rosemary
5 grams thyme
5 grams sage
5 grams basil
5 grams oregano

Make sure the olive oil is at least room temperature or slightly warmer. Wash and dry the herbs. Put the herbs into the whipping siphon. Pour the olive oil into the whipping siphon.

Seal the whipping siphon, charge it, and swirl for 20 to 30 seconds. Let the siphon sit for 1 minute longer. Place a towel over the top of the siphon and slowly vent it.

Strain the herb-infused olive oil and let sit for at least 5 minutes before using.

CHILE PEPPER-INFUSED PEANUT OIL

I really like the flavor of dried chile peppers and infusing them into oil adds great versatility to them. This oil works well as a topper for a stir fry or as a finishing sauce on a fajita.

I've used ancho and guajillo peppers because I enjoy the smokiness they add to the oil but feel free to use any dried peppers you like. This recipe also works well with fresh peppers.

Ingredients
225 grams peanut oil
20 grams dried ancho peppers
15 grams dried guajillo peppers

Make sure the peanut oil is at least room temperature or slightly warmer. Wash and dry the chile peppers then cut them into strips or coarsely chop them. Put the chile peppers into the whipping siphon. Pour the peanut oil into the whipping siphon.

Seal the whipping siphon, charge it, and swirl for 20 to 30 seconds. Let the siphon sit for 1 minute longer. Place a towel over the top of the siphon and slowly vent it.

Strain the chile pepper-infused peanut oil and let sit for at least 5 minutes before using.

INFUSING VINEGARS

I love adding a bit of brightness to dishes through a splash of vinegar just before serving. I've found that using infused vinegars is a great way to introduce that brightness but complemented with great flavors. Infused vinegars are also excellent when used in vinaigrettes or sauces.

RASPBERRY VINEGAR

My wife loves raspberry vinegar on salads but most decent ones are pretty expensive. I use this recipe to inexpensively make my own at home. I can whip up a batch in just a few minutes and if I double the recipe I have plenty to last for several weeks. Try to use a decent vinegar since it will greatly affect the final taste of the infusion.

For an easy vinaigrette just blend this infusion with some salt and pepper and 3 parts good olive oil.

Ingredients
230 grams white wine vinegar
60 grams raspberries

Make sure the white wine vinegar is at least room temperature or slightly warmer. Wash and dry the raspberries then put them into the whipping siphon. Pour the white wine vinegar into the whipping siphon over the raspberries.

Seal the whipping siphon, charge it, and swirl for 20 to 30 seconds. Let the siphon sit for 1 minute longer. Place a towel over the top of the siphon and slowly vent it.

Strain the raspberry vinegar and let sit for at least 5 minutes before using.

CHIPOTLE PEPPER VINEGAR

This vinegar infusion has a smoky spiciness that is great drizzled over meat or fish. It can also be used in salad dressings for an additional kick. Feel free to add more chipotle pepper if you like a spicier infusion. You can use any of your favorite chile peppers in this recipe to create spicy vinegars with different flavor profiles.

Ingredients
230 grams white wine vinegar
20 grams chipotle peppers in adobo sauce

Make sure the white wine vinegar is at least room temperature or slightly warmer. Put the chipotle peppers into the whipping siphon. Pour the white wine vinegar into the whipping siphon over the chipotle pepper.

Seal the whipping siphon, charge it, and swirl for 20 to 30 seconds. Let the siphon sit for 1 minute longer. Place a towel over the top of the siphon and slowly vent it.

Strain the chipotle pepper vinegar and let sit for at least 5 minutes before using.

Infusing Vegetables and Fruit

In addition to infusing liquids with flavored ingredients, the process can also work in the opposite direction. Pressurizing porous ingredients with a strongly flavored liquid will infuse the ingredients with the flavor from the liquid.

This can be used to quick pickle vegetables, marinate meats, or even make unusual flavor combinations such as celery infused with apple cider.

This recipe uses the infusion process to quickly make sweet pickles. It uses a very standard sweet pickle recipe but any pickling liquid will work. I use it here on cucumbers but it will work with most crisp vegetables such as radishes, celery, onions, or squash. For less porous vegetables such as carrots or beans, let it sit for an extra 30 minutes or so.

For ease of use, cut your cucumbers so they easily fit into and out of the mouth of your whipping siphon.

Ingredients
For the Brine
200 grams water
200 grams cider vinegar
300 grams sugar
8 grams kosher salt
5 grams mustard seeds
3 grams coriander
2 grams celery seed
2 grams turmeric

For the Pickles
½ sweet onion, thinly sliced
1 medium cucumber, sliced 6mm / ¼" thick

For the Brine
Combine all the ingredients for the brine in a pot and bring to a boil. Stir until the sugar and salt dissolve completely. Remove from the heat.

For the Pickles
Add the onion and cucumbers to the still-hot brine. Let the brine cool then pour it and the vegetables into the whipping siphon, being sure not to overfill it. Seal the siphon, charge, and shake well. Let the siphon stay pressurized for at least 20 to 30 minutes, either in the refrigerator or on the counter.

Vent the siphon then pour out the pickles into a bowl. The pickles are then ready to serve.

Pickled cherries are a great way to add a nice tart sweetness to many richer dishes. I especially like them on fattier cuts of meat such as seared duck breast, braised short ribs, or pork belly. You typically would use bing cherries but any sweet cherries will do.

Ingredients

For the Brine
125 grams water
200 grams red wine vinegar
200 grams sugar
18 grams kosher salt
10 grams whole peppercorns
3 grams whole coriander seeds
1 cinnamon stick
10 grams orange zest
2 grams cloves

For the Cherries
225 grams sweet cherries

For the Brine

Combine all the ingredients for the brine in a pot and bring to a boil. Stir until the sugar and salt dissolve completely. Remove from the heat.

For the Cherries

Add the cherries to the still-hot brine. Let the brine cool then pour it and the cherries into the whipping siphon, being sure not to overfill it. Seal the siphon, charge, and shake well. Let the siphon stay pressurized for at least 20 to 30 minutes, either in the refrigerator or on the counter.

Vent the siphon then pour out the pickled cherries into a bowl. The cherries are then ready to serve.

BLOODY MARY CELERY

Celery is a great carrier of other flavors due to its mild flavor. Modernist Cuisine uses apple juice to create apple flavored celery but most strongly flavored liquids can be used. Here I create a Bloody Mary flavored celery that can be eaten by itself or as a garnish for drinks such as a vodka martini.

Ingredients

2 cups Bloody Mary mix
1 celery head, cut into long pieces

Combine all the ingredients in the whipping siphon. Seal the siphon, charge, and shake well. Let the siphon stay pressurized for 20 to 30 minutes, either in the refrigerator or on the counter.

Vent the siphon then pour out the celery into a bowl. The celery pieces are then ready to serve.

SECTION FOUR

CARBONATING

The third major whipping siphon technique is to carbonate liquids and other foods. Most whipping siphons work just fine with the CO2 cartridges used in soda siphons and this gives all liquids in the siphon the classic fizzy taste. It can be used to make sparkling sodas and drinks, or for a fun twist you can carbonate foods like grapes and watermelon.

General Carbonating Process

Whenever you are carbonating something, the general process is the same. Simply chill the liquid or food you want to carbonate and then put it into the whipping siphon and seal it. Charge the siphon with CO2 and let it sit for a few hours, typically in the refrigerator, to fully carbonate.

The exact amount of time needed will vary on the type of food you are trying to carbonate. Most liquids take one to two hours while fruits and vegetables can take up to twelve hours.

Once it has sat for a while, vent the CO2 from the whipping siphon. You can then open the siphon and serve the carbonated liquid or food. Most liquids will stay carbonated for up to an hour and fruits will typically stay

carbonated for 10 to 30 minutes.

How Carbonating Works

Carbonating a liquid or moist food works very similarly to how creating foams with N2O does. A liquid is sealed in a whipping siphon and CO2 is forced into the siphon. The CO2 is absorbed into the liquid over time while it is under pressure in the siphon. Once the liquid is no longer under pressure, the CO2 slowly emerges from the liquid, giving it the fizzy, carbonated taste and mouthfeel.

CO2 only dissolves in cold liquids, so chilling the liquid is critical to carbonating it.

Carbonating Tips and Tricks

There are several tips and tricks to keep in mind when you are carbonating liquids or foods.

The Colder the Better
Carbonation works much better on cold liquids because the CO2 is more readily absorbed. Because of this it is usually a good idea to chill anything you are going to carbonate before putting it in the whipping siphon.

However, frozen foods also will not carbonate.

Faster Carbonating

For faster carbonating you can clear out the air from the whipping siphon. To do this, after you seal the siphon, hold down the dispenser to vent the gas right away as you charge it with a CO_2 cartridge. This will take most of the air out of the siphon. You can then charge the siphon normally and the time needed to carbonate will be reduced.

Sour Taste

Sometimes things that have been carbonated can take on a sour taste. This is because the sour receptors in our mouths are activated by the carbonation and give the sensation of sour. This flavor can usually be masked with some sugar or fruit juice.

CO_2, Not N_2O

When carbonating, make sure to use CO_2 charges because the CO_2 stays in foods longer. N_2O escapes almost immediately, leaving a foam behind but no carbonation.

CARBONATING LIQUIDS

Using CO2 cartridges with your whipping siphon allows you to carbonate almost any liquid you want. It's an excellent way to make sparkling beverages ranging from orange sodas to sparkling cocktails.

The carbonation process is very easy. Simply add the liquid to the whipping siphon, charge with CO2, and let sit for at least an hour or two. Vent the CO2 and then pour out the carbonated liquid.

Sometimes the CO2 can add a slightly bitter taste to drinks. When this isn't desired it can be covered up through the addition of some sugar or fruit juice.

CUCUMBER AND SOUR APPLE SODA

There are unlimited combinations of juices that you can carbonate and turn into sodas. One of my favorite combinations is cucumber and sour apple. It is nice and light and also healthy because there is no sugar added. Of course, if you prefer sweeter drinks you can always add some honey or agave nectar to the juices.

To create the juices either use a juicer or puree the cucumbers and sour apples in a blender or food processor and strain out the juice. Some higher-end grocery stores also sell fresh juices.

Tools Needed
CO2

Ingredients
250 grams cucumber juice
150 grams sour apple juice
Honey or agave nectar, optional

For Garnish
Cucumber slices
Mint leaves

Combine all ingredients in the whipping siphon. Seal the siphon and charge with one CO2 cartridge. Vent the whipping siphon then fully charge with CO2. Place in the refrigerator for at least one to two hours.

When ready to serve, fill two glasses with ice. Vent the whipping siphon. Open the siphon and pour out the soda into the glasses. Serve with a slice of cucumber and a mint leaf or two.

Variation: Vodka Spritzer

This soda also works well as the base for a vodka spritzer. You can add the vodka before or after carbonating the juices. I'll often fill a glass with ice and the soda then top it off with some vodka.

SPARKLING APPLE CIDER

This is a simple recipe that showcases how easy it is to make carbonated beverages with a whipping siphon. It can be adapted for use with most liquids and fruit juices.

I often use a variation of this recipe to create different flavored juices, either to drink alone or as mixers in cocktails. Most fruit juices work well, especially cranberry juice or orange juice and the carbonation gives drinks made with them some lightness and extra flavor. For instance, my wife loves cosmos made with carbonated cranberry juice and carbonated tequila sunrises are an usual take on the classic drink.

Tools Needed
CO2

Ingredients
Enough apple cider to fill your siphon to the fill line

Chill the apple cider then add to the whipping siphon. Seal the siphon and charge with one CO2 cartridge then vent the whipping siphon. Fully charge the siphon with CO2. Place in the refrigerator for at least one to two hours.

When ready to serve, vent the whipping siphon. Open the siphon and pour out the sparkling cider.

Variation: Sparkling Amuse Bouche

For a fun variation you can blend in 0.5% xanthan gum with the apple cider at the start of the recipe. Once the cider has been carbonated you can either vent it or dispense it as you normally would for a foam.

The resulting carbonated liquid will be much thicker and you can serve it as a soup-like amuse bouche.

Old Fashioneds are sometimes made with club soda. While purists might not approve, it can be a nice and refreshing take off of the classic drink. In this recipe I actually carbonate the drink itself instead of watering it down with club soda. This recipe will make enough for 2 to 3 drinks but you can always scale it up to make more.

Another benefit of the carbonation process is that much of the flavor of the orange peel is pulled out into the cocktail.

Tools Needed

CO_2

Ingredients

1 teaspoon sugar
Several dashes Angostura bitters
6 ounces bourbon or rye
3 pieces orange peel

For Garnish
Twists of orange or lemon peel

Combine all ingredients in the whipping siphon. Seal the siphon and charge with one CO_2 cartridge. Vent the whipping siphon then fully charge with CO_2. Place in the refrigerator for at least one to two hours.

When ready to serve, take Old Fashioned glasses and add ice if desired. Vent the whipping siphon. Open the siphon and pour out the sparkling Old Fashioned into the glasses. Serve with a twist of orange or lemon.

SPARKLING MOJITO

Mojitos are a great summer cocktail and carbonating them just adds to the refreshment. You can make your own mojito mix or use your favorite packaged mix.

For the recipe below, I prefer to make a mint simple syrup so the mint and sugar is more evenly distributed but in a pinch you can just add all the ingredients to the siphon to start with.

First make the mint simple syrup. Place the sugar, mint, and water in a pot. Heat to a boil, stirring, and cook until the sugar is dissolved. Set aside and let cool. Pour through a strainer.

Combine the mint simple syrup with the remaining ingredients and mix well. Taste and adjust the lime juice, sugar, and alcohol levels to taste.

Pour into the whipping siphon. Seal the siphon and charge with one CO_2 cartridge. Vent the whipping siphon then fully charge with CO_2. Place in the refrigerator for at least one to two hours.

When ready to serve, fill glasses with ice. Vent the whipping siphon. Open the siphon and pour out the sparkling mojito into the glasses. Serve with the mint leaves and lime slices.

Tools Needed
CO_2

Ingredients
60 grams sugar
10 mint leaves, coarsely chopped
160 grams water
200 grams rum
75 grams lime juice, preferably fresh

For Garnish
Mint leaves
Lime slices

CARBONATING FRUITS AND BERRIES

A fun use of the carbonation process is to make carbonated fruits and berries. It's a great way to add unique mouthfeel to common foods and to surprise your diners. Like all whipping siphon carbonating, the CO2 is introduced to the liquids in the fruit through the whipping siphon.

The fruit can be placed into the siphon whole or cut into pieces. The more exposed surface area, the faster it will carbonate, and also the faster it will lose its carbonation.

The carbonation may also mask some of the sweetness of the fruit due to its stimulation of the sour receptors.

Carbonation Process

The process of carbonating fruits and berries is very simple. First chill the fruit, this will help with the CO2 absorption. Add the fruit to the whipping siphon. Seal the siphon and charge with CO2. For faster carbonating, you can vent the first CO2 charge to expel the air at the top, then charge the siphon again.

Once charged, refrigerate the whipping siphon for at least an hour and up to overnight. The amount of time needed for the food to carbonate will be dependent on the size of the fruit and how much surface area it has. The carbonating time will also determine how carbonated the fruit becomes and how long the carbonation will last in the fruit.

When you are ready to serve the fruit, simply vent the CO2 from the siphon and open it. The fruit is then ready to serve. Most fruit will stay carbonated for 10 to 20 minutes but some may last for several hours.

Best Bets for Carbonating

Some classics items to carbonate are grapes, cherries, orange or tangerine segments, and pieces of cantaloupe, watermelon, banana, tomato, apple, and cucumber.

Some berries do not carbonate well, such as strawberries which take on the same mouthfeel as spoiled strawberries.

Another thing you can carbonate is modernist spheres. They will take on the carbonation very well.

Tips for Carbonating Fruits

Here are some tips for carbonating fruits and berries.

Preventing Split Skins

Grapes and other items with skins can sometimes burst. You can cut them in half to alleviate this problem. You can also add liquid to the whipping siphon and it will help prevent the bursting.

Surface Area and Carbonation Time

The carbonation is absorbed through the moist surface areas on the fruit. The more surface area there is, the faster the carbonation will be absorbed and the quicker the process will take place. For instance, a grape cut in half will carbonate much faster than a whole grape. However, the carbonation will also leave more

quickly so be sure to serve these foods as fast as possible.

Add Additional Flavor

If you add liquids to the whipping siphon when carbonating fruits the flavor from the liquid will infuse the fruit. This allows you to make fun variations such as apple cider grapes.

Chill the Fruit

Because cold liquids absorb carbonation much more readily it is a good idea to chill the fruits before you carbonate them. This will not only speed up the carbonating process but it will also ensure the fruit is more fully carbonated.

CHERRY TOMATO AND CUCUMBER SALAD

Tomatoes and cucumbers both take well to being carbonated. They are also a good flavor pairing. I combine them with a champagne vinaigrette, mozzarella cheese and basil for a nice summer salad.

You can also carbonate the mozzarella which, due to it's high water content, holds the carbonation really well. The slight sourness of the CO2 also complements the flavor of the mozzarella.

Tools Needed
CO2

Ingredients
1 pint cherry tomatoes
1 cucumber, cut in half and then half moons

For the Champagne Vinaigrette
62 grams champagne vinegar
1 shallot, diced
1 garlic clove, minced
Salt and pepper
165 grams olive oil
2 tablespoons chopped mint leaves

For the Salad
Small mozzarella balls or diced mozzarella
Toasted croutons
Basil leaves
Salt and pepper

Place the tomatoes and cucumbers in the whipping siphon. Seal the siphon and charge with one CO2 cartridge. Vent the whipping siphon then fully charge with CO2. Place in the refrigerator for several hours or preferably overnight.

For the Champagne Vinaigrette
Combine the vinegar, shallot, garlic, salt, and pepper in a bowl. Let sit for 5 minutes. Blend in the olive oil with an immersion blender or whisk. Stir in the mint leaves.

To Assemble and Serve
When ready to serve, vent the CO2 from the whipping siphon. Place some tomatoes and cucumbers into a bowl. Dress with the champagne vinaigrette. Top with the mozzarella cheese, croutons, and basil leaves. Season with salt and pepper and serve.

The tomatoes and cucumbers will usually hold their carbonation for 10 to 20 minutes.

Variation: Vinaigrette Froth
For a fun variation, you can blend 0.25% to 0.5% xanthan gum into the vinaigrette. Then once you remove the tomatoes and cucumbers you can quickly make a froth. Pour the vinaigrette into the whipping siphon, seal and charge with N2O. During the assembly of the salad dispense the vinaigrette on top of the salad.

CARBONATED GRAPES

Grapes are the go-to item when people start experimenting with carbonating fruits. You can use either green or red grapes, depending on what type of dish you are serving them with. You can cut them in half for faster carbonating but they will also lose their carbonation faster.

There are many uses for carbonated grapes. They are great as a component on a cheese plate. You can use them as a garnish on a cold gazpacho or fruit soup. They are also a nice amuse bouche in between courses.

This recipe can also be used with most types of fruit or berries you'd like to carbonate.

Tools Needed
CO2

Ingredients
Enough grapes to fill your whipping siphon to the fill line

Chill the grapes and place in the whipping siphon. Seal the siphon and charge with one CO2 cartridge. Vent the whipping siphon then fully charge with CO2. Place in the refrigerator for several hours or preferably overnight.

When ready to serve, vent the CO2 from the whipping siphon. Pour out the grapes and serve. They will hold their carbonation for 10 to 20 minutes.

Sangria is a great summer drink and the fresh fruit in it always adds a nice touch. For this recipe I carbonate the fruit that goes into the sangria for some added brightness and mouthfeel. I've included a recipe for sangria but feel free to use your favorite red or white sangria recipe and any fruits you prefer.

Tools Needed
CO2

Ingredients
Orange segments
Apple chunks
Peach chunks
Grapes

For the Sangria
1 bottle red wine
¼ cup brandy
½ cup triple sec
¼ cup simple syrup
½ cup orange juice
¼ cup lime juice

Chill the fruit and place in the whipping siphon. Seal the siphon and charge with one CO2 cartridge. Vent the whipping siphon then fully charge with CO2. Place in the refrigerator for several hours or preferably overnight.

For the Sangria

Combine all ingredients in a pitcher and stir well to mix. This can be done ahead of time and stored in the refrigerator for several hours or over night to chill.

When ready to serve, vent the CO2 from the whipping siphon. Pour the fruit into the sangria and serve. The fruit will usually hold their carbonation for 10 to 20 minutes.

FIZZY WATERMELON SALAD

With all the water in watermelons they carbonate really well. I like the flavor of watermelon with mint and jalapeño. It's a nice combination that is light and refreshing but still full of flavor.

Tools Needed
CO2

Ingredients
Enough watermelon chunks to fill your whipping siphon to the fill line

For the Salad
Lime wedges
Mint leaves, cut into thin strips
Jalapeño, thinly sliced into rings
Salt and pepper

Place the watermelon in the whipping siphon. Seal the siphon and charge with one CO2 cartridge. Vent the whipping siphon then fully charge with CO2. Place in the refrigerator for several hours or preferably overnight.

To Assemble and Serve

When ready to serve, vent the CO2 from the whipping siphon. Place some of the watermelon into a bowl. Squeeze a lime wedge over the watermelon. Top with the mint leaves and jalapeño. Season with salt and pepper and serve.

The watermelon will usually hold its carbonation for 10 to 20 minutes.

CARBONATED FOAMS

Another fun use of carbonation is to create fizzy foams. To create these just follow the standard processes for making a foam in the whipping siphon but use CO_2 instead of N_2O. Carbonated foams work very well for desserts or drinks. However, they tend not to work well with most meats or other savory dishes.

Quick Recipe: Fizzy Raspberry Foam

Combine 400 grams raspberry juice, strained, and 2 grams xanthan gum (0.5%) with a blender until the raspberry juice has thickened. Pour into a whipping siphon, seal, and charge. with CO_2. Let sit in the refrigerator for several hours to fully carbonate and then dispense as needed.

CARBONATED YOGURT

You can also carbonate other liquids such as creams or yogurts. The sour notes from carbonation tend to go well with the natural sourness of yogurt. Just carbonate the yogurt as you would any liquid. It's good as part of a tzatziki sauce or plain over fruit and berries.

SECTION FIVE

REFERENCES

INGREDIENT TABLES

I am always adding more ingredients to my website. Come by and see what I've been using lately.

You can find it on the website at:
www.modernistcookingmadeeasy.com/info/
modernist-ingredients

INGREDIENT TECHNIQUES

Ingredient	Emulsions	Foams	Gels	Spherification	Thickening
Agar		X	X		
Carrageenan: Iota		X	X	X	X
Carrageenan: Lambda	X	X			X
Carrageenan: Kappa			X		
Gelatin		X	X		
Gellan	X	X	X		
Guar Gum	X				X
Gum Arabic	X	X			X
Konjac	X		X		X
Lecithin	X	X			
Locust Bean Gum			X		X
Maltodextrin					X
Methylcellulose	X	X	X		
Mono and Diglycerides	X	X			X
Pectin	X	X	X		
Pure Cote B790			X		
Sodium Alginate			X	X	
Ultra-Sperse	X	X			X
Ultra-Tex	X	X			X
Versawhip		X			
Xanthan Gum	X	X			X

INGREDIENT TEMPERATURES

When you are trying to determine which ingredient to use, the hydration, setting, and melting temperatures can be very important.

Ingredient	Dispersion	Hydration	Gel Sets	Gel Melts
Agar	Any	100°C / 212°F	40-45°C / 104-113°F	80°C / 175°F
Carrageenan: Iota	Cool	Above 70°C / 158°F	40-70°C / 104-158°F	5-10°C / 9-18°F above setting
Carrageenan: Kappa	Cool	Above 70°C / 158°F	35-60°C / 95-140°F	10-20°C / 18-36°F above setting
Gelatin	Above 50°C / 122°F	Cool	30°C / 86°F	30°C / 86°F - 40°C / 104°F
Lecithin	Any	Any	N/A	N/A
Maltodextrin	Room temperature	N/A	N/A	N/A
Methylcellulose:				
Methocel F50	Any	Below 15°C / 59°F	Above 62-68°C / 143-154°F	Below 30°C / 86°F
Methocel A4C	Hot	Below 15°C / 59°F	Above 50-55°C / 122-131°F	Below 25°C / 77°F
Mono and Diglycerides	Above 60°C / 140°F	Any	N/A	N/A
Sodium Alginate	Any	Any	Any	Above 130°C / 266°F
Xanthan Gum	Any	Any	N/A	N/A

HOW TO USE GELATIN

If you are interested in staying up to date with modernist cooking you can join our free newsletter and get monthly modernist cooking tips and links to the best articles on the internet.

You can join our newsletter here:
http://is.gd/Jwiwij

Gelatin is one of the oldest "modernist" ingredients in western cooking. It is used in many childhood favorites from the ubiquitous Jell-O at family picnics to the marshmallows roasted in s'mores.

HYDRATING GELATIN

All gelatin has to be hydrated, or "bloomed", before it can be used. Gelatin commonly comes as a powder or in dry sheets. They are both used in a similar manner but have a few differences when hydrating.

Hydrating Powdered Gelatin

To hydrate powdered gelatin you sprinkle it in cold liquid and let it sit for 5 to 10 minutes. The gelatin and all the liquid will go into the recipe and should be taken into account.

Hydrating Gelatin Sheets

Gelatin sheets are also hydrated in a cold liquid for 5 to 10 minutes. However, once they have hydrated you squeeze the liquid out of the sheets and it does not go into the final recipe.

DISPERSING GELATIN

Once the gelatin has been hydrated you need to disperse it into the liquid you want to gel. This is typically done through whisking, either by hand or with an standing or immersion blender.

When dispersing the gelatin make sure the liquid is warm, typically above 50°C / 122°F. If you don't want to heat all of the liquid you can dissolve the gelatin in a portion of it and then combine it with the rest. You can also disperse it in water first and then mix it into the flavored liquid, though it will dilute the flavors some.

CONVERTING BETWEEN GELATIN TYPES

As mentioned previously, there are two main types of gelatin, powdered and sheet. Sheet gelatin also comes in four different strengths: bronze, silver, gold, and platinum. The strength of gelatin is measured by their "bloom strength" and each type of sheet gelatin has a different bloom strength. I've listed them, as well as Knox, the most popular brand of powdered gelatin, in the table below with their bloom strength.

However, because of the difficulty in moving between gelatin types I tend to have both powdered gelatin and sheet gelatin on hand so I can use whatever a specific recipe calls for and save myself the effort of converting.

Type	Bloom	Grams / Sheet
Bronze	125-155	3.3
Silver	160	2.5
Gold	190-220	2.0
Knox Powdered	225	-
Platinum	235-265	1.7

Because the sheets of gelatin are different sizes, they actually contain the same amount of gelling power. So if a recipe calls for "1 sheet of gelatin" you can use any type of sheet.

Powdered gelatin typically comes in ¼ ounce / 7.2 gram packets of 225 bloom strength. Four sheets of gelatin equal about one packet, so each sheet is around 1.8 grams.

If you are using a recipe that calls for 2% powdered gelatin, you can figure out the number of sheets you need to use for every 100 grams of liquid by dividing the percent by 1.8. However, this only works for small amounts because the math isn't exact and at larger volumes the small differences add up.

For a detailed look at this conversion process I highly recommend reading an article by Daniel R. Moody that goes into detail explaining how to convert from one type of gelatin to another. You can find the article on Daniel's blog: http://danielrmoody.com/2012/01/08/powdered-vs-sheet-gelatin-converting-between-the-two/

Modernist Cooking Resources

For an up to date look at current books, websites, and other modernist cooking resources you can visit the list I keep on the website.

You can find it at:
www.modernistcookingmadeeasy.com/info/
modernist-cooking-resources

Modernist cooking is a very complex process and there is a lot more to learn about it in addition to what has been covered in this book. There is more and more good information available about modernist cooking. Here are some resources to help you continue to expand your knowledge.

Modernist Cooking

Books

Modernist Cooking Made Easy: Getting Started
By Jason Logsdon

If you are looking for more information about the other modernist techniques then my first book is for you. It will give you the information you need to create gels, foams, emulsions, as well as teach you how to do spherification, thickening, and sous vide cooking. It also has more than 80 easy-to-follow recipes to get you on your way.

Beginning Sous Vide: Low Temperature Recipes and Techniques for Getting Started at Home
By Jason Logsdon

My main book covering sous vide. It deals a lot with the various equipment options and has over 100 recipes, some of which have been specially adapted for this book. It is available from Amazon.com or on my website as a paperback or Kindle book.

Modernist Cuisine: The Art and Science of Cooking
By Nathan Myhrvold

This aims to be the bible of modernist cuisine. It's over 2,400 pages costs $500 and was several years in the making. If you are serious about learning the newly developing modernist techniques then this might be worth the investment. It can be a dense read, and many of the dishes are very complicated but for sheer quantity of information it can't be beat.

Modernist Cuisine at Home
By Nathan Myhrvold

A much more accessible version of Modernist Cuisine especially written for the home cook.

Alinea
By Grant Achatz

A beautiful, picture-filled book with amazing techniques and whimsical dishes. Great to use to find inspiration for your own dishes.

Sous Vide Grilling
By Jason Logsdon

My book that is focused on grilling and BBQ recipes. It includes 95 great recipes covering steaks, burgers, kebabs, pulled pork, and everything in between. It is available from Amazon.com or on my website.

Sous Vide: Help for the Busy Cook
By Jason Logsdon

My book focusing on how to use sous vide around your busy schedule. Full of recipes, tips and tricks to make sous vide work for you.

Ideas In Food
By Aki Kamozawa and H. Alexander Talbot

Delve into the "why" of traditional and modernist cooking.

Texture - A hydrocolloid recipe collection

Compiled by Martin Lersch from Khymos.com, is a great compendium of recipes for many modernist ingredients.

On Food and Cooking
By Harold McGee

This is the ultimate guide to the scientific aspects of cooking. If you like to know why things happen in the kitchen, you will find this book fascinating.

Cooking for Geeks
By Jeff Potter

If you are interested in the geekier aspects of cooking then this book does a great job. It takes you through the basics of setting up your kitchen all the way up to kitchen hacks and sous vide cooking.

Websites
Modernist Cooking Made Easy
http://www.modernistcookingmadeeasy.com/

My website is full of recipes, tips, and tricks for modernist cooking. It also has forums and other ways to talk with other passionate cooks.

Cooking Sous Vide
http://www.cookingsousvide.com

This is the main website where I contribute sous vide articles. I update it regularly with original recipes and news from around the sous vide community. There are also community features such as forums and question and answer pages.

Hydrocolloids Primer
http://www.cookingissues.com/primers/hydrocolloids-primer/

Dave Arnold and the Cooking Issues website help to clarify some of the uses of and reasons for modernist ingredients.

Apps

I have two sous vide apps for the iPhone and iPad available, as well as one for the Android. You can search in the app store for "Sous Vide" and mine should be near the top, published by "Primolicious".

INGREDIENT AND TOOL SOURCES

Many of the modernist ingredients cannot be picked up at the local grocery store. I have had good luck on Amazon but here are some other good resources to find these ingredients.

Modernist Pantry
https://www.modernistpantry.com

Modernist Pantry has a good selection of ingredients and equipment. I tend to buy most of my ingredients through them.

Molecule-R
http://www.molecule-r.com/

Molecule-R has a good selection of packaged ingredients and tools. Their ingredients tend to be a little more expensive but if you are just getting started then their Cuisine R-Evolution kit can be a good way to get many of the ingredients and tools to get started.

WillPowder
http://willpowder.net

WillPowder has a decent selection of the more common ingredients.

RECIPE INDEX

I am constantly adding recipes to my website as I continue to
experiment with modernist cooking.
Maybe something there will inspire you.

You can find them at:
www.modernistcookingmadeeasy.com/info/modernist-recipes

DID YOU ENJOY THIS BOOK?

If you enjoyed this book check out my other books on modernist cooking.

Modernist Cooking Made Easy: Getting Started

If you are looking for more information about the other modernist techniques then my first book is for you. It will give you the information you need to create gels, foams, emulsions, as well as teach you how to do spherification, thickening, and sous vide cooking. It also has more than 80 easy-to-follow recipes to get you on your way.

Beginning Sous Vide

My main book covering sous vide. It deals a lot with the various equipment options and has over 100 recipes, some of which have been specially adapted for this book.

Both books are available from Amazon.com as both a paperback and Kindle book.

ABOUT THE AUTHOR

Jason Logsdon is a passionate home cook, entrepreneur, and web developer. He helps cooks understand new modernist cooking techniques with easy-to-understand directions and recipes. He has several books and websites on modernist cooking that are read by thousands of people every month including *Modernist Cooking Made Easy: Getting Started, Beginning Sous Vide*, and *Sous Vide: Help for the Busy Cook*. His websites are www.ModernistCookingMadeEasy.com and www.CookingSousVide.com. He can be reached at jason@modernistcookingmadeeasy.com or through Twitter at @jasonlogsdon_sv.

Made in the USA
Columbia, SC
17 June 2023

17883009R00074